DAVID'S ADVENTURE WITH SCHIZOPHRENIA

MY ROAD TO RECOVERY

All the Best

KENT

DAVID LaCHAPELLE

"A JOURNEY OF A THOUSAND MILES
BEGINS WITH A SINGLE STEP."

—LAO-TZU

CONTENTS

DAVID'S ADVENTURE WITH SCHIZOPHRENIA

INTRODUCTION

One person in one hundred will develop Schizophrenia. You may be suffering from Schizophrenia or know somebody who is. If so, this book will comfort you that you are not alone or will make you aware of what a loved one may be going through. Maybe you just want to read a true, action-packed story full of surprises and humor. If so, then *David's Adventure with Schizophrenia* is the book for you. This story is about two undiagnosed individuals who lead each other across the great country of Canada and briefly visit the United States of America on a mission to save the world. Throughout the characters' journeys, it seemed that a guardian angel was watching over them both as they encountered many spiritual, exciting, and peculiar situations.

The characters stayed out of harm's way by using craftiness to survive despite having access to very few little resources. David was in and out of hospitals, mental hospitals, and jails yet for the most part did not receive proper treatment. The ignorance of society is seen throughout the book as the systems of two countries failed the characters, and an unfortunate event had to occur for the main character to be able to receive the care he so desperately needed. In this book, you can expect to receive insights into the characters' thoughts, paranoia, delusions, and feelings about the events and people they encountered. You will also discover how hard it is for a person with Schizophrenia to recover, but that it is possible to get better if you take your medication.

I was inspired to write this book because the story of that part of my life had to be told. The moment I entered into a recovery stage, I had thoughts about writing this book, but I could not attempt it because it was too painful. Over time, writing my story became therapeutic, and I shared it with family and friends. After one year of hard work, my story is finally complete and available to you. Enjoy!

PART ONE

ON THE RUN

CHAPTER 1

MEETING ANGELA

In 1996, when I was twenty-three years old, I moved from Toronto to Ottawa to attend Carleton University. In my first year, I was registered in the electrical engineering program and lived on the second floor of the Lanark residence hall. I took political science electives and engineering courses at the same time. I discovered that politics was more interesting and fun. During my second year, I transferred to the political science program and volunteered at Parliament Hill. I loved politics so much that I wanted to be the prime minister of Canada. I lived off campus for the rest of my time at school and enjoyed the independence of being on my own.

Throughout this life transition—being away from home and emerging into adulthood—I slowly started to feel different than I had before, but I could not explain why. The problem was that the students at Carleton did not know me before, but they witnessed the deterioration of my mental health and were concerned. It was not until the summer of 1999 that I entered a full-blown psychotic state. I was frightened, because I did not know what was happening to me. I could feel negative energy from others, and I blamed others for my wounded condition. I was paranoid of others, because this energy felt awful, and there was nothing I could do to stop it.

I then became confidently arrogant to compensate for my insecurity and the fear I felt inside. I could not function in society anymore and that is when my world started falling apart. I was expelled from Carleton in the same year, after having been on two years of academic probation. I lost my part-time office-worker job at The Brick furniture, appliance, and electronic superstore. I started to isolate myself from family and friends and ended all communication with them. My family came up from Toronto to observe my living conditions and state of health. My family suspected I might be suffering from Schizophrenia because my late Aunt Patricia had the illness. My friend Mike Purves who previously lived next to my room in residence, on the other hand, had no clue and came to visit me at my apartment, which was a rare thing for him to do. I always visited Mike at his apartment because I had a car and he lived a fair distance away from me. The bottom of my life had just dropped out, so I agreed with my family that I should come back home.

When I arrived in Toronto, I rejected the family's invitation to live with my mother. I took off in a hurry from my mother's apartment complex and drove all around town. During the daytime, I used my car in an attempt to intimidate the city folk in their vehicles by driving extremely close to their bumpers, and I slept in my car at night. I kept to this schedule for approximately one week until I realized that my efforts were not changing the fear I felt inside. I called my mother collect from a payphone in Toronto. I did not say too much as I was really ill. My family traced that call and found out that the call originated from the Danforth area, near downtown Toronto. My mother lived in the suburbs, so I was a thirty minute drive away from her place. The next night, I decided to visit the Emergency Department at North York General Hospital. The chief psychiatrist interviewed me to determine if I qualified for admittance to the hospital. Unfortunately, my answers to his probing questions brought him to the conclusion that I did not require psychiatric help. I had told him, "I am not paranoid; I do not hear voices in my head." Clearly, I was mentally ill, but the psychiatrist went only on my own interior thoughts about my mental health, even though I was not in a position to judge my condition.

After this hospital experience, I decided that I had to heal myself by meditating. I spent most of my time at the beaches on the shores of Lake Ontario to meditate in the sun. After I meditated for a few days, my hard work finally paid off, and a feeling of enlightenment was cast upon me. I decided that now would be a good time to visit my mother and brother at their apartment. When I entered the apartment my mother and brother desperately served me food, they were very concerned about me. I thought at the time they were being so nice to me because they were scared as a result of my spiritual power.

I called my friend Lannie, my ex-roommate in residence at Carleton University in Ottawa, and I told him, "I can heal you, Lannie" (grandiose delusion). My mother talked to him and then I left the apartment. I went back to the beaches again and stayed there day and night. During the day, I tried to intimidate people I thought were evil by staring at them. At night, I slept in my car in the parking lot. I did this for a couple of weeks until I realized that there were too many evil people and that I could not save the world with my own power. I decided that if I was going to have more power, I must be endowed with power from above. My plan was to go to church and declare among the patrons that I am the savior of the world. I thought that my holy coronation would boost my spiritual powers and end the madness that was going on in my world. In the morning, I went to the People's Church and sat and listened to the sermon while crying profusely. After the service, I went down to the pulpit. Two gentlemen approached me and asked me what I needed. I replied, "I am looking for refuge."

One gentleman, whom I thought was evil, asked me, "Do you want physical or spiritual refuge?"

I did not answer him, and that is when the other gentleman, named Mathias, took me to the back room and I accepted Jesus Christ as my savior. It was a very spiritual moment that I will never forget. The moment I signed my life over to Jesus Christ, I felt that I was a new creature. I was born again. The new spiritual instructions, which descended from above, in an enveloping blanket of love, replaced my old way of thinking. It felt as if Jesus were watching from his throne to authorize this holiest of transactions. It was as if I were revitalized with a new spirit and given a fresh start in life. The first step of my new life was to be invited to Mathias's apartment, where he gave me some milk and cookies and asked me if I would like to go to his daughter's house for lunch. At his daughter's house, we ate sandwiches and talked about politics.

The next day, I went to my mother's apartment to get some food. While I was there, my father and brother showed up with two police officers with a Form 2 (a Form 2 is a legal affidavit, for placing individuals, who are a recent threat to themselves or others, to a mental hospital for 72 hours for treatment) from the Justice of the Peace. The police officers handcuffed me, placed me in the back of a police cruiser, and took me to North York General Hospital. I was placed in a holding room under police supervision. While there, I told the police officer, "I am being persecuted by my mother. Look at your records. My mother has called the police on me numerous times for no particular reason" (persecutory delusions). The police officer guarding me ignored my rambling, and a few moments later, I was transferred to another holding room, where a nurse injected Haldol (an older antipsychotic agent) into my arm. I had an immediate reaction and had difficulty breathing, so I requested some water. After I took a drink, my breathing passages opened up again. The next thing I remember is waking up in the middle of the night, realizing that I was strapped to a bed and that a mental health worker was outside my room looking through a Plexiglas window and taking notes on my behavior.

The next morning, the staff opened the door of the holding room and directed me to my new room, which was on the same ward. My roommate was a young fellow in his early thirties. He was recovering from an attempted suicide, having taken an overdose of prescription medication, and he was very fragile emotionally. He was jealous that Angela, a patient on the ward, had taken a liking to me and not to him. My male nurse had said about Angela, "Stay away from her; she is big trouble." Angela left gifts at my room door and always wanted to talk to me. One time, I told her to get lost because she was hounding me so much, and she then cried for a couple of minutes. I liked Angela, and there was instant chemistry between us; I felt as if I had known her my whole life.

A billboard at the nurses' station, I noticed, displayed my visitors' log. I saw my mother's name on the log, and this infuriated me. I immediately expressed my feelings to the nurses: "I do not want any visitors." The nurses ignored my initial requests, and shortly after, my mother was allowed into the ward to visit me. While my mother was waiting for me in a room, I went up to the nurses' station and screamed, "I do not want any visitors." I hid in my room until they removed her from the ward. I called my friend Mike Kostin a few moments later and told him he could visit me. That night, he arrived at the hospital, and I gave him the keys to my car, which was parked in front of my mother's apartment complex. Mike took my vehicle to his parents' place and unbeknownst to me, my family reported my car stolen.

I arrived at the hospital on a Thursday in the late afternoon and saw my doctor Friday morning—and never saw him again until his weekend holiday was over. This left me in a state of limbo. When I saw the doctor, it was a Tuesday, and he spoke to me for only a minute, just like the first time I met him. After I'd been neglected for a week in the hospital, Angela introduced me to her lawyer and recommended that she help me get out of the hospital too. I hired her immediately, and during our first meeting, she said

5

she could get me out with no problem. Angela gave me her home phone number, telling me, "David, when you get out the hospital, call me and we will order Chinese food at my place, because I am getting out of the hospital in a couple of days."

I told my friend Mike that I was getting out of the ward soon. He said, "David, you can live at my parents' house when you get out of the mental ward."

Within a few days, I had a patient hearing, which would be a forum for the board members to listen to my request to be released from the hospital. My father supported the doctors' position that I should stay in the hospital, but he showed up reeking of alcohol and was not taken seriously. Mike and his family, on the other hand, came to the hearing and supported my view that I should be released from the hospital. The board agreed with my lawyer that my doctor had never documented in writing that he'd informed me of my rights. My rights were that after a seventy-two-hour period, I could accept treatment or not. If I refused treatment, then I was free to leave. The doctor acknowledged that he had made a mistake, but it was too late.

In retrospect, I don't see the purpose of having a patient hearing to begin with, except that the board members wanted to assess my condition before my release. When the meeting adjourned, I immediately became an undiagnosed free man. Unfortunately, when I was released from the hospital, I was very ill. My mind was scrambled and I was mentally exhausted. I could not function and I think Mike's family was only slightly aware that something was not just right with me. Anyhow, it took them only a week to realize that I was really sick, and they wanted me to move out of their place. They had even promised the hospital board they would take care of me; they thought at first that my mother probably *was* out to persecute me because they had witnessed her ill treatment of me. When they examined the situation more closely, however, they probably realized that they had made a mistake by inviting me into their home.

Out of sheer desperation and curiosity, I called Angela at her home, and that night I picked her up at her downtown apartment. We bought some take-out at a hamburger place, and I went back to her place, where she seduced me. The next morning, Angela informed me that it was her last day at the apartment. I do not know if she was being evicted or if she had given her notice to vacate the unit. We decided to go for a drive in my car and see where it would take us. We drove to London, Ontario, and while driving there, I became overwhelmed and could not focus on the road. Angela told me, "Angels are all around us, Dave, and it is OK to let go of the steering wheel." I let go of the steering wheel and I guess she was right, because it seemed the car drove itself for a minute or two (hallucination). Miraculously arriving in London in one piece, we stayed at a motel, where the motel clerk insisted on giving us the honeymoon suite, which had a heart-shaped tub in it. We had to leave that night because Angela was paranoid that a guy by the name of Chris was following us and would soon catch us at the motel. What this guy Chris would do to us I was not really sure, but Angela was frightened of this man for some reason. I only found out after the fact that Angela also had Schizophrenia, but at the time, I was consumed by her fears and followed her every whim.

We arrived in Niagara Falls in the late evening, when it was dark outside. As soon as I arrived, I became extremely ill and paranoid. I was full of fear and thought that the sightseers walking along the river's path were actually walking dead people (hallucination). This alarmed me and forced me to take evasive action. I decided that we had to get out of the downtown core, where most of these creatures seemed to lurk. I then drove erratically, breaking many traffic laws, until we ended up in the country. I was glad that my driving tactics had successfully freed us from the bondage of the enclosing dead. Unfortunately, the path that I took led us directly to the side of a graveyard. Angela then began to freak out, and she started shouting at me, "Why did you take me to a graveyard?" My confidence was shattered. "David," Angela continued, "get me away from here."

We made our way to the main street, back into enemy territory. Angela noticed a police station. "Pull into the police station," she commanded. I pulled into the station reluctantly, not seeing the purpose of going to the police. Angela jumped out of the car the second I stopped my vehicle and parked at the back of the station. She started running toward the police station. I was unaware that she was about to tell the police officers that I had physically assaulted her, so I walked into the front entrance of the police station. I hadn't done anything wrong, and I thought that Angela had an important reason to run to the police station. I did not know that she wanted to get rid of me.

I waited in the hallway for a few minutes and was then taken to a room to be interviewed by a police officer. The officer asked me, "Did you physically assault Angela?"

"No," I replied.

The police officer questioning me seemed bewildered, because to him I seemed to be answering his questions sincerely. A few moments later, the same police officer instructed me, "You better leave without Angela."

In complete and utter disbelief about what had just happened, I hung out at a donut store parking lot by the highway and pondered my next move. I decided to drive back to Toronto, and as I was driving there, I held a Bible out of my sunroof to ward off what I thought were evil people on the highway. Arriving in Toronto, I decided to sleep in a motel for two nights and paid for the room with my Visa credit card. I used the motel just for sleeping and spent most of my waking hours at the beach. When checking out of the motel, I became infuriated because the bill was $600—all because I had used the motel's phone to talk long distance for some time with my friend Lannie, in Ottawa. At the time, I'd been unaware that motels charge so much to talk long distance.

I couldn't afford to stay at the motel, so I lived out of my car in beach parking lots. The first day back at the beaches, I decided to bathe in Lake Ontario. While I was in the water, a black military helicopter that looked like an Apache hovered just over me. Right away, I thought that I must be an important person (grandiose delusion) and that the good people of the Earth were worried about me. I thought they must have sent this aircraft to watch over me to make sure that nothing bad happened to me (delusion: ideas of reference). The helicopter, now that I look back in time, was probably for the Toronto Air Show, which was taking place not far from where I was bathing. While living at the beaches, I met a homeless man named Jacob, and again as I look back in time, I think he must also have had Schizophrenia. At the time, I thought I was Jesus, and because Jacob acknowledged me by saying, "Hello" when I walked by him, I thought he must know who I was. I slept in his tent for a night and found comfort in somebody who had thoughts similar to mine.

The next day I went to a grocery store in Scarborough, a suburb of Toronto, to buy some food. There, I ran into an old high school friend by the name of Chris, and he invited me back to his townhouse. At his place, I ate the food I bought, ate some of his food, drank a beer, and smoked some cigarettes, even though I was a nonsmoker at the time. I somehow sensed that his wife was evil, so I left his place with little notice and went back to the beaches.

I succeeded in reaching Angela on her cell phone the next day. She told me, "I miss you, David. You can pick me up at the YWCA [Young Woman's Christian Association] in Kitchener, Ontario."

CHAPTER 2

TRAVELING WESTWARD

I arrived in Kitchener in the evening and from a local donut store parking lot called Angela on my cell phone to get directions to the YWCA. A few minutes later, I arrived in front of the shelter. Angela excitedly ran to greet me. "How are you, Dave?" she asked. Later, she said, "Let's go back to Toronto, Dave."

In Toronto, we had no particular destination to attend to so Angela asked softly, "How far is Vancouver?"

"Vancouver is pretty far," I explained. Angela and my-self then had a quiet mutual agreement that traveling to the West Coast was our best bet. We traveled north all the way to Newmarket, Ontario, where we decided to stop at a local grocery store. It had been Angela's idea to get some food, so I sent her into the grocery store; at the time, I was really sick and I was tired from all the driving I'd done. When Angela came out of the store, she said, "The grocery clerks were making a fuss about you."

"How come?" I asked.

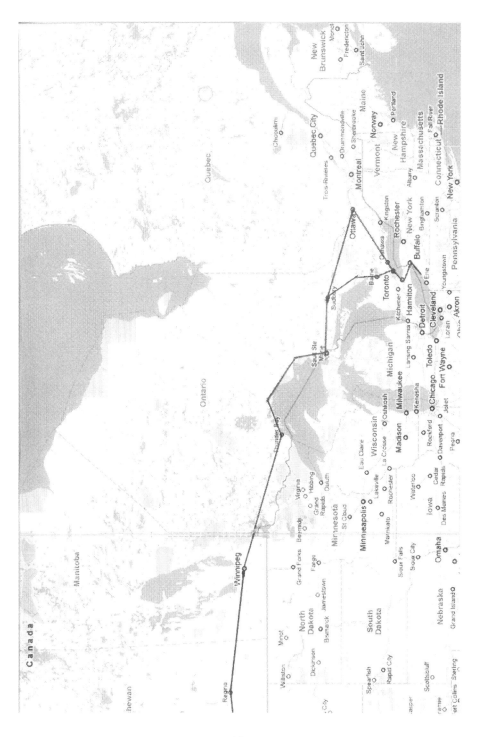

She said that the clerks had said, "Oh! David is here." Angela made me feel like a celebrity, and I thought to myself that I must be an important person for the clerks to know who I was without ever meeting me (grandiose delusion).

We traveled north to Parry Sound, Ontario, into the heart of the province, and rested in the McDonald's parking lot for a couple of hours that night. We felt safer there because in that area there were not a lot of people to foster our overwhelming paranoia. Angela, however, suspected that so-called evil people would catch up with us and that if we did not leave soon, they would soon catch us (delusion). We proceeded north to Sudbury, Ontario, where we filled up on gas and continued westward to Sault Ste Marie. In between Sudbury and the Sault, we slept in the car at a truck inspection station. It was early August 1999, and although it was a bit chilly at night, we were still able to sleep in the car. I drove from the Sault in the daytime toward Thunder Bay, Ontario. In Thunder Bay, I called my financial institution to see if I could sell some of my Eaton's stock to get some money. I kept driving northwest and ended up in Ignace, Ontario, at night. It was pretty cold there, and we slept in the car at a Tourist Centre parking lot. I filled up some empty bottles with water available from a tap connected to the outside of the building complex.

The next morning, while Angela was calling her mother from the restaurant/gas bar, I exchanged my jar of change for some gas. The jar was mostly pennies, and the gas attendant gave me a funny look. He reserved his judgment, and we went on our way. We drove northwest toward Dryden, Ontario, arriving during daylight hours. I decided to sell my diamond gold ring, worth $300, for about $20 at a pawnshop. We bought some more gas and headed northwest toward Kenora, Ontario. We arrived there at night, and our first stop was the local indoor shopping mall. The mall was pretty small, so it did not take long to walk through the entire mall. The locals seemed bewildered to see strangers. We parked outside a McDonald's and slept through the night. The next morning, we ventured to downtown Kenora. I noticed float planes taking off and landing on the lake. I found another pawnshop and sold my CDs and a few knickknacks for about $40.

Realizing that we still needed more money, I called my friend Mike at his home to ask him to wire me some via Western Union. Mike's mother answered the telephone and told me Mike was not home. I then left a message with Mike's mother that I was in Kenora and needed some money wired to me. After talking to her for a few minutes, she told me through her silence that she was not going to help me.

We left Kenora and soon after arrived in Winnipeg, Manitoba. We rested in a KFC parking lot, where Angela told me, "Dave, you should sell your car." I drove by the used car dealerships to sell the car but was not able to enter a dealership to sell the vehicle. The reality was that I did not want to give up my beautiful 1992 Navy Blue Honda Accord EXR. I doubted that Angela's motives were sincere, and I did not see how we would survive without a vehicle. I was also overwhelmed and foggy because I was suffering from the unpredictable fluctuations of an unattended mental illness. I was full of fear and confused as to what to do. My senses were overloaded because I was hallucinating, and I was beginning to shut down mentally. It did not help that Winnipeg was a busy town; the more people we had to deal with, the more paranoid we became. We were right in the middle of rush hour, so to get some security and tranquility in our minds, we left the city of Winnipeg immediately.

Our journey took us westward to a little town just outside of Winnipeg called Portage la Prairie, Manitoba. By the time we entered this town, our funds were depleted, and we were low on fuel. We stayed there a couple of rainy nights so that I could strategize what I would sell to garner us enough money to get us moving again. I was stuck as to what to do because I somehow wanted the journey to continue without making any sacrifices. I did not want to sell my prized possessions, but Angela was threatening to leave me, calling her father on her cell phone to ask him to fly her home. I wanted her to continue the mission, because I did not want to be all alone in the middle of Manitoba.

After the second night, I sold my leather school bag and electronic organizer for about $40. This gave us enough money to get moving again, and we drove to the outskirts of Brandon, Manitoba. It was a late Monday afternoon in Brandon, where I got some good news: Some money had been deposited in my bank account from the sale of my Eaton's stock. I bought some fuel, but Angela and I argued about what we were going through. Angela wanted to be with me, but at the same time, she wanted to leave me. After we bought a couple of Subway sandwiches, which Angela refused to eat, she reluctantly agreed to continue the journey.

We arrived in Regina, Saskatchewan, at dusk. We bought some more fuel and headed westward toward Moose Jaw, Saskatchewan. Between Regina and Swift Current, Saskatchewan, we were pulled over by the Royal Canadian Mounted Police (RCMP). I received a ticket for reckless driving, because I had passed a car while speeding over a double line. The police officer took me back to the cruiser, while another police officer interviewed Angela by my car. They eventually discovered that Angela had been reported kidnapped by her mother in Ontario. We had to go back to the police station, where they aggressively interrogated Angela in a room as I waited patiently on a bench in the hallway. They released Angela after fifteen minutes, and then we had to wait because the police officers were not finished inspecting my vehicle. After a few minutes, a police officer told us, "Your car is ready" and escorted us out of the station. Back in the car, Angela and I laughed about what happened, and I think it brought us closer together than ever before.

We arrived in Swift Current late in the evening and drove straight westward toward Medicine Hat, Alberta. We drove throughout the city to check it out, and because it was so late at night, it was like a ghost town. We left Medicine Hat unable to find an open restaurant or store. I kept driving although I was hungry; in the early morning hours, we arrived in Calgary, Alberta. We stopped at a McDonald's for some breakfast and drove through downtown to take in the sights. I wanted to check into a hotel or motel to get some sleep, but Angela kept telling me to keep going, so I did. On the outskirts of Calgary, between the city and the mountains, we pulled into a gas station/restaurant to buy some gas and two chicken dinners. I noticed a helicopter flying nearby, and I thought it was following us. I became impatient with Angela because she was taking so long to get our food, so I went into the restaurant to investigate. I figured the people in the restaurant must be working in conjunction with the helicopter to slow our progress because they were evil (delusion: ideas of reference).

We knew we were exiting the Calgary area when we saw the Rocky Mountain range. The picturesque town of Canmore, Alberta, a little town nestled between the foothills of the Rocky Mountains, greeted us first. There were shops in the middle of this tiny valley, and houses surrounded that valley. We delved deeper into the Rocky Mountains, and it seemed the paranoia I once had disappeared. We made our way to Banff, Alberta, where a few elk on the road seemed undisturbed by our presence. After our encounter with nature, we stopped into town to purchase some more fuel, and in the early evening, we made our way toward British Columbia. I drove all the way to Kelowna, British Columbia. By this time, I was completely exhausted and passed out in my car for a couple of hours in the Tim Horton's parking lot.

When Angela woke me up, she said, "Dave, I was spiritually fighting off devils [patrons at the Tim Horton's] all night." She also told me it was not safe to stay there any longer. Still groggy from my interrupted nap, I drove

16

down the highway to get away from our troubles. I drove far enough to be out of the town, but I was so tired that I just collapsed. Thankfully, there was a rest stop right in my path. I did sleep at this rest stop for a few hours, although Angela did not want me to. When I woke up at the rest stop, Angela told me she'd had to spiritually fight off the truck driver who was in his truck beside us (hallucination). I awoke somewhat refreshed from my nap and wondered if something was wrong with Angela, because on both occasions I did not see the threats she perceived. Then, unsure about Angela, I drove my car through the mountains like a racecar driver all the way to Merritt, British Columbia.

CHAPTER 3

VANCOUVER AND THE FRASER VALLEY

We eventually made our way to Maple Ridge, British Columbia, just on the outskirts of Vancouver. While getting our room, Angela was determined to bargain for a lower rate, and she succeeded. The next day, I walked to a grocery store, where I bought my main food staple: frozen lasagna. The room where we stayed had a kitchen, which was a bonus. I cooked the lasagna and then we ate. During the night, Angela started to freak out. She was convinced there was blood on the floor (hallucination), but upon later inspection, we discovered it was just tomato sauce. During one afternoon, we drove to where my cousin Kent used to live and where I had lived for a couple of months a few years earlier. I showed Angela where I carved my name in the concrete in the visitor's parking space. We next drove around town aimlessly, and Angela noticed a large movie theatre. She asked me if we should see a movie. I replied, "Sure. I know a movie you will love." That evening, I took her to see *Star Wars: Episode I - The Phantom Menace.*

Angela was amazed by the movie and said, "Dave, we must be Jedi knights, and you must be Anakin Skywalker" (grandiose delusion).

The next day, we went to the welfare office to get some money, but they kicked us out by calling two police officers: We insisted on getting some money immediately. They told us, "You have to go to a welfare meeting in some other location a few times in order to get a check." We decided to attend this meeting the next day, and the meeting was about how to look for and obtain employment. We needed money instantly, and this method did not seem promising, so we left the meeting early and never went back. Then I remembered that my old employer, "The Brick," still owed me one paycheck and vacation pay. I called my old employer's Human Resources department, and they told me they needed my address so they could send the check.

A light bulb went off in my head that I needed to open a mailbox at a postal store. I looked in the Yellow Pages and saw that there was a mailbox store on Cambie Street. Angela and I immediately ventured to this store, and I opened up a mailbox. I then called my old employer and gave them my new address in Vancouver. They told me it would take a couple of weeks before I received the check. By this time, we needed money badly, so we drove to a used car dealership and traded my 1992 Honda, which had 125,000 km on it, for a 1992 Buick Regal with 250,000 km on it and$1,000. The salesperson told me, "We cannot make a deal until Saturday," and at the time it was late Friday. I therefore sold my car stereo to a pawnshop for $50.

During this time, we tried to sleep in the car, but we didn't realize we were in a rough area of town. Out of nowhere, two prostitutes approached my window and babbled some loud, obnoxious noise, which scared us. Shortly thereafter, a police officer showed up and asked me, "What are you doing in this area?"

I replied, "We are getting some rest after a long journey."

He then said, "This is not a good area. You better go somewhere else."

We followed his advice and went to Surrey, British Columbia, where we tried to sleep in the parking lot of an outdoor mall that was home to a popular bar. It was Friday night, and because the bar was busy, we realized it was not a good place to sleep until we could trade my car. We were awakened by a guy and his male friend, who stood right in front of my car and started screaming, "I think I am going crazy" while holding his head. We immediately left, and I drove around Surrey until I found a quiet parking spot at a large indoor mall parking lot.

During our stay in Surrey, I noticed a man in his car, which was gleaming with light from inside. I said to Angela, "Look! There is a man who is holy and is on our side" (delusion: ideas of reference). Now that I look back in time, I realize that he probably just had his interior lights on in his vehicle.

We ended up at the dealership on Saturday morning, and while I was getting my insurance, which in British Columbia is government insurance, the agent seemed a bit weird. I confirmed my cousin's address, where I'd lived when I owned my previous vehicle. I vividly remember that day: The insurance agent was talking proudly on the phone, or so it seemed; somehow, his conversation was accidently put on speakerphone, and I discovered he was talking to a dial tone.

We used the money I received from the trade to stay at the London Guard motel in the Kingsway area of Vancouver. I remember exiting the motel room our first morning to get some food. As I veered across the street, I noticed a short lady burning a mysterious object in an old coal barbecue. While this barbecue was on fire, she performed some kind of ritual dance. I thought it was black magic against us because we were staying across the street from her (delusion: ideas of reference). For that reason, we stayed there only a couple of nights. During the day, we drove around town to discover what the area had to offer. We came upon English Bay, a residential area by the ocean. While there, I noticed an "Apartment for Rent" sign, and I convinced a reluctant Angela to look at the available suites. We toured one of the units, but when the superintendent quoted the price, I knew I could not afford it. We needed a stable place to live; this dream was out of reach, and we moved on.

Disappointed, we went to the beach and talked about what to do next. I whispered because I did not want anyone else to hear our conversation: I thought people were spying on us. Angela complained that she couldn't hear what I was saying. She asked me, "Are you Jesus?"

After a delay, I said shyly, "Yes" (grandiose delusion).

"Do you know where I am from?" she asked.

I did not say anything because I revered her in this moment, when she seemed powerful.

She answered her own question: "I am from the ocean" (grandiose delusion). Angela turned toward the ocean with a wave of her hand and commanded, "Be quiet." It seemed that the once noisy and wavy ocean instantly became quiet and still (hallucination). I then became scared of Angela because I thought she had special powers. At the same time, I was glad she was on my team.

We next drove around town and ended up going through Port Moody. We were low on fuel, so I looked for a gas station and I spotted one, but there was a problem: Four RCMP cruisers were parked at the pumps. I wanted to avoid the police at all costs. I noticed another gas station up the hill, but I was too late; the car decided at that moment to run out of gas. We were able to coast toward this gas station, but after being refueled, the car still would not start. Realizing we could not leave the car conked out at the gas station, I coasted down the road. I parked beside a train station. The car was immobile, so to get a little cash I decided to sell some of my philosophy books at the used bookstore.

We lived in the car at the side of the road for a few days. We were getting hungry, and our situation was desperate, so we took a long walk. We ended up at a Zellers department store in a shopping mall. I decided to get a Zellers credit card since I had good credit. We took advantage of the card's limit of $1,000 that day and bought food, cosmetics, gold rings, and things I thought I could sell. We made it back to the car and slept there all night. The next day, we went for a thirty-five-minute walk to the mall in Coquitlam. Our first stop was The Bay, where I signed up for a Bay card and bought some clothes.

After that, we went to the Future shop to get a credit card there. While waiting at the front checkout for our credit application to be approved, Angela noticed a Muslim woman dressed in her abaya (black robes), and Angela, being Persian in descent, yelled at her in English, "What are you doing at Future shop?" Angela was infuriated that this woman from the old country was actually buying something at a modern store that was full of the latest electronics. My credit application was denied, so we went across the street to a local bank, where I tried to get a credit card. The tellers at the bank did not cooperate and answer my questions, so I thought they were evil. To irritate them, I called 911 from the customer phone in the bank. When they learned I had called 911, they became angry with me, and we were told to leave.

On our way back to the car, we walked by a Canadian Tire Store. A sign in the window indicated the business took personal checks. At that moment, I remembered that I had brought my personal checks out West with me. Checks in hand, I bought a battery charger and some snacks. We walked to the car and ate our snacks, and I charged the battery overnight in the train station terminal's electrical outlet. Unfortunately, the car would still not start in the morning. In the afternoon, two police officers showed up and told us to move on, so we did. While we were walking with all our stuff from our shopping trip, the male officer accused, "You stole all of these items."

I countered, "Back off. I paid for them."

He then threatened me. "I can arrest you." I calmed down, and then he let us go. He told us, "I am going to tow the car."

The next step was to find a place to sleep. We stayed all night in the ATM area of a bank. It was warm, but in the early-morning hours, two police cruisers containing four officers arrived and told us, "You guys better move on." Hoping to find another place to stay, we hopped on a bus to downtown. While walking downtown, I almost passed out on the street because I'd eaten so little. We needed money, so I sold the watch I'd bought at Zellers for $10; the pawnshop took it for $30. We ended up walking along Hastings Street late at night and almost got mugged, but we walked fast and crisscrossed the street to evade the creature that was following us.

Eventually, we made our way to a downtown shelter, but it was full. The lady working the shelter's front desk recommended we try to get into another free shelter near the University of British Columbia, in an area called Jericho Beach. We took her advice and walked there. I was carrying some of my belongings in a large plastic bag. I ditched them in the bushes at the side of the road because the shelter was nowhere in sight and I was tired from carrying the bag. We walked down a side road and finally saw the hostel through the mist in the distance. We were disappointed again: The shelter turned out not to be free.

We ventured back to the main road and hopped on a bus for free to downtown Vancouver, eventually ending up at the YWCA. We were grateful that they took us in and that they told us we could stay as long as we needed. We thought we had it made, until we received a phone call after being at the hotel for only two hours. It was Friday, and we would have to leave by Monday. That Monday, we had nowhere to go, so we tried to sleep under a roof by some offices. That didn't go over so well with the Vancouver Police. The officers were going to take us into custody, but when they realized I had a local address, they let us go. What they did not realize was that my local address was just a mailbox.

Dumbfounded as to where to go, we wandered around downtown at nighttime. We wanted shelter but had no money. I went to the Salvation Army with Angela, but they did not allow females into the shelter. Angela was not prepared to leave me because she would have to go to a nearby women's shelter. We wandered a bit more, and then Angela instructed me to check my bank account. She informed me, "You have $120 in your bank account." I then went to an ATM to check my balance, which was indeed $120, and I withdrew the money. To this day, I do not know how she knew this. She could not have deposited the money because she was with me twenty-four hours a day. Anyhow, this was enough money to get us out of the rain, and this time we paid to check into the YWCA for a couple of nights.

After our stay, we took a bus trip to North Vancouver to visit Capilano Mall, where we tried unsuccessfully to obtain a Sears credit card. Unsatisfied that one cashier had rejected us, we went to another one in a different location in the department store. I did not take no for an answer from the second cashier and demanded an explanation. Security showed up and pressured us by their presence to leave the department store. Angela and I took a bus back to the downtown core. We accidently ended up at the Simon Fraser University downtown campus, where warmed up a bit to get out of the rain.

Angela surprised me by saying for the first time, "David, you are sick; call your mother." Late that evening, I called her collect from a payphone. Because of the time change, it was really late where she was, and I probably woke her up. My mother was speechless during our one-sided conversation as I informed her that I was in Vancouver. My family thought I was still residing in Toronto at the house of my friend Mike's parents.

The next morning, we wandered up to the mailbox place, hoping to find a $900 check from my old employer there. Hooray! It was there. We walked a fair distance to downtown, where we cashed the check at Scotiabank. While we were touring downtown on foot, Angela insisted we get married (she noticed we'd passed a marriage registration office). We took the elevator up to the office, and I paid the $100 to register. I was very wary of marrying Angela, but I purchased the license anyhow. Angela said, "If we get married, the devils of the world will be off of our backs and will leave us alone."

Angela's marriage proposal was all motivated by a wedding dress that she had spotted earlier in a bridal store window and liked. We went to the US Consulate General and tried to become US citizens. After we waited for ten minutes, they called security and kicked us out. Angela and I booked a hotel on the outskirts of downtown. We ate some Hungry Man TV dinners that I bought down the street at a grocery store. We crashed on the bed, but an earthquake in the middle of the night interrupted our sleep.

We had to find a cheaper place to stay, so we ended up staying two nights at the Best Western Plus on Granville Street, in the entertainment district. During our stay, I worked my magic to find out where my car was and how to get it free. I made a few phone calls to the right people and eventually discovered where my vehicle was impounded. When my cab arrived at the impound yard, I noticed that my car was at the back of the lot surrounded by a maze of other vehicles. The man in charge told me, "I can't get your car out today because there are too many other cars around it."

I said, "You better get it out or else."

This motivated him to free my car in about three minutes. I hopped into the tow truck as my car was being towed to the mechanic, who said, "I can fix your vehicle, and I will include the towing service bill in the repair bill."

The tow truck driver was starting to freak out because he wanted his money. I told him the mechanic would pay him, and he settled down. Having straightened things out, I met up with Angela at the hotel and told her the good news. She was happy, and the next day we picked up my repaired car, which had suffered from a blown fuel pump. We then picked up the bag I had ditched in the bush, and then we headed east.

CHAPTER 4

TRAVELING EASTWARD

I drove all night eastward toward Chilliwack, British Columbia. After getting take-out at a Wendy's restaurant, we entered the Rocky Mountains. While we were driving through the mountains that morning, Angela sensed that a vehicle that was speeding dangerously around the corner toward us might collide with us. The tractor-trailer almost clipped the front of my car at high speed, and its tires threw a rock at my windshield and chipped it. A little shaken from our close encounter, I kept driving until we arrived in Banff, Alberta. I called my mother collect and asked her to wire some money via Western Union. I told her we were close to Thunder Bay, Ontario, even though we were not, and I requested she send the money to the Thunder Bay Western Union location. After eating at McDonald's and gassing up, we left for Saskatchewan.

The RCMP in Saskatchewan pulled us over in the same location as the previous time. It was kind of funny because we encountered the same officer who had pulled us over on the way to Vancouver. I immediately said, "Hello!" and "How is it going?" and "Do you remember me, Officer?"

The officer did not respond and went right to his cruiser. I did not know what was in store, although I was confident everything would go smoothly because I hadn't broken any laws. I realized it was just a routine check. Then, the loudspeaker of the police cruiser behind me unexpectedly blasted out a loud question from headquarters: What would the officers like on their pizza? I thought that was the funniest thing as Angela inquired as to why I was chuckling to myself. The police officer released us without giving us a ticket or any suggestions, and then we made our way out of Saskatchewan.

Well into Manitoba, we ended up outside of Brandon that night. I wanted to go into Brandon to get some gas, which was just off the TransCanada Highway One, but I did not know how far away the town was, so we kept driving. Just down the road from the Brandon exit, we ran out of gas. I panicked but then spotted a small gas station. I walked there with my Jerry can to get enough gas to start the car. I let a Good Samaritan drive me back to my car because it was wet and cold outside, although I was suspicious of someone doing me a favor. After putting in the little bit of gas I'd gotten, I drove to the gas station and filled up the tank. I had spilled some gas on my hands from using the Jerry can, so it was hard to eat the spicy potato chips I bought at the station.

Our next stop was Winnipeg, where an ATM ate my CIBC Visa card. I felt a big void in my heart. We passed by Kenora, Ontario, and kept going east until we hit Dryden, Ontario, in the early morning hours. We did four loads of laundry in this pulp and paper mill town, and once we changed into our freshly cleaned clothes, we proceeded southeast to Ignace, Ontario, in the afternoon. I called my mother collect to see if she had sent the money to the Western Union in Thunder Bay. I was glad to hear that she had, and we picked up my funds at the local Shoppers Drug Mart.

Although I felt newly rich, I thought the girls working at the store had an attitude. Out of disgust, I threw a penny by the store's entrance as if asking a penny for their thoughts. Angela told me, "Don't do it," but I did anyway because I was angry. We went across the street to Zellers to see if its restaurant was open, but it was not. Angela looked at some jeans at a small shop and then we ate at Taco Time in the food court. The Taco Time girl taking my order acted as if she were doing me a favor, so I reminded her that *she* was the one working at Taco Time, not me.

On our way out of town, the police pulled us over because a front headlight was out. I'd been unaware of that. The officer told me to fix it and then let us go. We then made our way to Sault Ste Marie, where I dealt with the headlight problem.

Between the Sault and Sudbury, I slowed down to let a car pass, but it kept following me. I stopped at the side of the highway, and the car behind me stopped, too. At the time, I thought I could hear the driver's thoughts in my head (delusion: thought insertion). I thought he was saying he wanted to kill us. When he finally passed us about five minutes later, I chased him and came close to running him off the road. He pulled into a Tim Horton's, and I followed him. Planning to confront him, I waited for him in my car. He went into a convenience store, and I changed my mind about confronting him; I thought I'd scared him enough already.

We arrived at our next stop, Parry Sound, Ontario, at night. While driving on the highway, I noticed a vehicle tailgating me, so I did a U-turn to get away from the car. Soon enough, however, I realized the vehicle following me was a cop car. The Ontario Provincial Police pulled me over, and the officer ticketed me for driving dangerously and with a suspended license. I hadn't realized my license was suspended; that must have happened because of the tickets I received while living in Ottawa. I'd gotten these tickets because my vehicle registration number was registered to another vehicle. I'd bought my car at a Honda dealership in Toronto, and some funny business must have been going on there. After handing me the ticket, the male officer, backed up by his female counterpart, said, "You better not drive any-more." The two then left the scene.

Well, by this time, I knew that the officers were enticing me to continue driving without a license, but I did not know what else to do. I proceeded south down the highway, and—big surprise—the same police officers who'd just pulled us over were waiting for us. They arrested me for driving without a license and took us to the police station, where I was put in a holding cell. Angela spent her time in the local medical hospital, because Angela's mother was contacted by the police when I was arrested, and she advised the police that Angela was suffering from a mental illness. Angela refused treatment, and spent the rest of her time wandering the streets. My car was impounded, so the next day, we took an evening bus to Toronto.

In Toronto, we stayed two nights in an area known for its long stretch of cheap motels: Kingston Road. Angela told me, "David, go and sell your possessions at the storage facility." I followed her instructions and sold most of my possessions to a guy who gave me cash for my TV, stereo, computer, alto saxophone, vacuum, microwave, and a few other things. I got about $1,200 for the lot, which was far less than what I paid for them.

We moved on to Sudbury, where we stayed at a motel for about a week. We used this motel as a home base so we could rescue my car from the Parry Sound impound yard. On the third day, I tried to pay my fines at the license bureau, where an older woman told me, "You can't pay your fines here."

I replied, "What do you mean I can't pay my fines here? This is the license bureau!"

Eventually, she got someone who knew how to use a computer so I could pay my fines and free my car from the impound yard. I arrived in Parry Sound late in the afternoon. Much to my dismay, the impound yard was closed, so I had to take an evening bus back to Sudbury. The next morning, I succeeded in paying the impounding fee and freeing my car. We headed south east to Ottawa, where I gave Angela a tour of the town and Carleton University. We then travelled south to Toronto, by taking a different route and bypassed the Parry Sound region.

CHAPTER 5

CLAIMING POLITICAL ASYLUM

We arrived in Toronto in the evening with very little money in our pockets. Purchasing bus tickets and paying for the motel in Sudbury for a week had exhausted most of the funds I had acquired from selling my worldly possessions. After our night's rest in the car at a parking lot outside a park, Angela told me, "Dave, go sell the car." I drove down the street from the park to the used car dealerships on Kingston Road and chose the largest dealer to sell my vehicle to. I ended up selling my Buick for $1,000. I then walked with the check to the bank, but they gave me a hard time cashing the check because I did not have a bank account with that particular bank. I ended up cashing the check at a Money Mart. I walked back to the dealership, where Angela was waiting, and asked the sales staff, "Can you call us a cab?"

The cabby arrived in no time, and we told the cab driver to take us to the downtown bus terminal. We did have some luggage, which he loaded into the back of the taxi. Although I sold most of my possessions at the storage facility, I did keep some of my life's possessions because I was planning to start a new life, wherever that might be. The luggage consisted of a tennis bag that was mostly full of clothes and my two framed college diplomas. I also brought with me my computer technician briefcase, which contained all of my electronic projects along with parts and tools that I created and gathered throughout my three years at Seneca College.

At the bus terminal, we hopped on a bus for Niagara Falls and arrived there in a couple of hours. We took a cab to a motel off the beaten track and stayed there a couple of nights. Then, we transferred to another motel, but we noticed that this new motel was situated beside a graveyard. That disturbed us, so we left immediately. We went to another motel and tried to stay there for a week. The lady in charge at this new motel tried to rip us off on the price by promising us one price and then charging us more, so we demanded our money back and left. We called another cab and went to another motel that was closer to the action. We stayed there a few nights, until Angela persuaded me to leave everything behind to go across the border to the American side of Niagara Falls.

While walking across Rainbow Bridge, I started crying profusely because I thought that our mission was complete and that our bondage to evil Canada would be soon over. At the American border facility, Angela went up to the border officers and told them her name was Angela White (although her name was really Angela Vakila). They almost let her pass through, but when they realized she was not Angela White, they immediately took her into custody. I was just waiting in the waiting area because I did not really want to cross the border and I knew Angela would get caught. When they found out I was with Angela, they took me into custody as well, but separately. They put me in a holding room for fifteen minutes and then took me to an informal office room to be interviewed by a customs agent.

I told the agent, "I would like to claim political asylum because all the evil people in Canada are trying to persecute me" (persecutory delusion).

The agent asked me questions about myself, and while answering him, I noticed he did not write down my statements accurately. He created an incriminating profile to suit his interests, which did not reflect the truth. He finished his profile of me, and because of his bias, I would not sign the declaration form. This angered the border official, and when we were finished, he put me back into my cell for a couple of hours. Then, two immigration officials put us in a van and drove us to a county jail in Mayville, New York.

At the county jail, they took our fingerprints, separated us, and placed me in a room to get changed into my orange jail uniform. They put me in another room to get tested for tuberculosis, and then for a couple of days they put me in a holding cell away from the larger population, until they figured where to warehouse me. I shared the holding cell with three rough-looking guys; they looked like criminals who committed petty crimes in order to have food and shelter provided to them. Across from my cell was another cell housing a guy whose vehicle was being investigated by the forensic crime unit for a terrible crime he had committed. He was really scared about what they were going to find. He started acting crazy so he would not be criminally responsible for his actions.

They transferred me to a cellblock containing four or five cells. Each cell had automatic doors with iron bars. The cellblock consisted of a tiny hallway parallel to the cells. This hallway had four or five tables with a chair on each side bolted down to the floor. I was locked up all night until 5:00 in the morning, until they woke us up for breakfast and told us, "Stand up for head count."

Since I would not jump up on my feet as quickly as they wanted—it was so early in the morning—they thought I was a hardcore criminal, and that angered the guards. I did not get much sleep while I was there because a large inmate, who had the remote control, watched the TV with the volume on high twenty-four hours a day. This large man approached me on the second day to lend me his folk manual on how to get yourself out of prison legally. Later, I found out that he was incarcerated because he raped and murdered a young girl.

On the third day, a muscular guy invited me to bunk with him because he would protect me from the other inmates. He also told me, "If you want, I could arrange for you to have a pass out of the cell block to have sex with the female guard."

I did not respond to that invitation and thought that was an odd suggestion.

The muscular guy I bunked with was arrested because he had been transporting automatic weapons and was caught by a highway patrolman. This guy was from Philadelphia, Pennsylvania, and the rest were from Jamestown, New York, and New York City. The inmates took to me early because I was good at playing chess, and they knew I was Canadian. They knew this because of my accent and because I finished my sentences with "Eh!"

On the third day, I also got interviewed by a nurse who examined my mental health. I then got a phone call from a government representative from New Jersey who handled political asylum claims. She asked, "Are you serious about your claim, because Angela is not?" If you were, I would have to fly all the way to Western New York."

I told her, "I am not serious," and the next day we were extradited to Canada. We went back to the motel where we had stayed before and tried to get back all of our possessions that we'd left behind. The motel manager charged us $150 to have our possessions back, which I reluctantly paid.

We then moved across the street to another motel and took it easy for a while. I then called my Aunt Fran to give her permission to sell my 1973 Volkswagen Beetle, which I had stored at her place, for $2,500 and to have the money sent to me via Western Union in Niagara Falls. It took a couple of days to get the money. Once I received the money, Angela and I took an afternoon bus back to Toronto.

CHAPTER 6

THE CLARKE INSTITUTE

We arrived at the downtown bus terminal just before dusk. We took a cab to a motel off of Kingston Road. At the motel, Angela told me, "David, we should try to make a baby. Having a baby would help protect us from evil people." After we made love, I panicked that we needed to find a more permanent place to live, because we were sick of living from place to place. In the paper, I saw an ad for a hotel that you could pay for by the month. That night, we immediately took a cab to the hotel and paid for the month. While staying at this hotel, Angela and I went for a walk on Yonge Street at night. When we were walking, I felt that enormous pressure was being placed on me by my downtown surroundings. Then, out of nowhere five fire engines with blasting sirens and blaring lights crossed right in front of us and then disappeared into the night. Immediately, my pressure was relieved, and a sense of calm overtook my-self. I saw that event like an omen coming directly from God that everything was going to be OK (delusion: ideas of reference).

After a couple of days, Angela left me because she did not want to be with me anymore. She was gone all day, and I did not know if she was ever coming back. I decided to call my old friend Chris. "Chris," I said, "come and meet me at my place because your family is in danger." At the time, I thought that Chris's family was in danger from evil people and thought that Chris was not evil.

When I met Chris and his friend, I immediately thought he and his friend were evil too, and I did not hesitate to tell them what I thought. At the time, my family did not know where I was, but that soon changed when Chris contacted my family, informing them of my condition and my whereabouts. Angela came back that night, and after a couple of days, she called the police on me because she thought I was committing suicide: I stayed in the washroom too long (hallucination).

The police realized nothing bad was going on, so they just left and told Angela, "David has a right to stay here because the hotel room is in his name."

The next day, Angela told me, "Dave, you have to leave the hotel because it is not safe." I gathered my things in my tennis bag with my tail between my legs and wondered where exactly I should go. But before I even had to make that decision, my mother and father intercepted me just outside of the hotel with two police officers. My parents had obtained another Form 2, and they had me taken to the Clarke Institute, a mental hospital.

At the Clarke Institute, I was ranting and raving at the police officers for having no right to hold me against my will. Then, all of a sudden, my parents were whisked away to a separate room, and all the staff came out of the office, which had a glass window facing the waiting area where I was seated. They had ignored me previously, but now I had their attention. When the ten staff members came out of the office, they brought with them a stretcher, and I volunteered to lie down in the stretcher. The lady taking charge of the event told me, "What would you prefer? A needle or take some pills?"

I opted for the pills, which I thought for sure were pills to euthanize me. As soon as I took the pills, I felt death upon me, and at that moment, I surrendered my will to live. The medication took effect quickly, and I became drowsy. I must have passed out for a couple of hours. I was awakened by what seemed an angelic voice, and that voice was Angela's. Angela asked me, "How are you feeling, Dave?"

"I feel dead," I said.

The staff got me up on my feet and walked me to my room. On my way there, I saw through my foggy eyes a very happy lady standing in the hallway, and that lady was Angela's mother. I slept all night in my room and then was awakened again by Angela in the morning when she brought with her two Pepsis and a box of Smarties for breakfast. Angela obtained access to my room because she claimed that she was my wife. That day, I had a meeting with administration to make my case that I was being persecuted. I was released a couple of hours later, without having my mental status confirmed, although I was mentally ill.

Angela and I walked up Yonge Street and stopped at the local Pizza Pizza. At the restaurant, everybody was looking at me because I was really ill. My senses were completely overwhelmed, and I missed many social cues in the restaurant. I had to be guided by Angela as to what to do, as I looked rough and felt out of place. Angela told me, "David, you look crazy."

We went back to our hotel and got a surprise visit from Angela's mother, but we did not answer the door because we were scared of her. Angela told me, "Dave, your mom is like a green spider, and my mom is more like a black spider in terms of how they strike with their evil power."

The next day, Angela and I took a cab to her mother's apartment for dinner. We ate some traditional Iranian food, and I played video games with Angela's son. After dinner, Angela's mother said, "You two can stay here," and then she left the apartment.

Angela said, "My mother told me she is going to come back with a shotgun to shoot you," which was not true. Angela gathered some of her clothes from the closet, and we left. I was scared, and my nerves were rattled with what Angela had told me, so as Angela was throwing her clothes over the bridge, because she was trying to rid herself of her past, I was full of adrenaline rushing through my body.

We walked for some time toward the Ontario Science Centre and as we were heading there, Angela said, "Dave, did you know that Muslims are trying to stop time in order to kill the people from the future?" Angela then added, "Dave, we are people from the future."

At the time, I thought she was crazy.

Then, she subtly pointed to a billboard sign that advertised a Muslim physics project that was trying to stop time.

After walking by the Science Centre, we took a bus downtown. Even today, I can clearly remember how ultra-sensitive my senses were when I got off the bus. My tongue was so sensitive that I could taste the air, and I felt so alive that I thought the world was ending (hallucination). I pondered being able to acquire a Porsche because the world would soon be over, and there would not be anybody around to stop me from owning one. All of a sudden, the aliveness that I'd once felt ended, and my dreams of owning a Porsche were dashed—because the world was not ending at that moment.

We walked back to the hotel from the bus stop only to discover that we had received our eviction letter and that we had to be out of there by morning. The next morning, we signed off of our lease. They charged us more because they charged us by the week for four weeks instead of by the month for one month. Then, because we'd burned the counter a bit with our hot plate, they charged us damage fees to replace the counter. I left in disgust, ripping up my college diplomas and leaving behind a nice wool coat. And then, I left my Electronic Technician tool case outside the hotel's main entrance.

We went to the bus terminal in downtown Toronto and took a bus to Ottawa to speak about our situation with the prime minister of Canada.

CHAPTER 7

VISITING OTTAWA

For some reason, the bus taking us to the nation's capital pulled into a truck inspection station along the highway to get further instructions from a police officer. I guess there must have been some accident on the road, but anyhow, I thought that was peculiar. I figured it was a safety precaution displayed by the good people of this Earth to protect us from evildoers—and to warn them that there was precious cargo on board: Angela and me (delusions: grandiose and ideas of reference).

When we arrived in Ottawa in the early evening, it was dark and cold outside because it was late October, 1999. We took a cab to a local medical hospital because Angela wanted me to get checked out. During the bus ride, she had told me that she saw blood in my urine at the hotel and that she was concerned. I went to Montford Hospital, where they ran tests on me for my so-called problem. The results came back in an hour or two, and the doctor told me that everything was fine. We took a cab from the hospital to the YWCA. On the way there, Angela started giving heck to the cab driver, accusing him of taking the long route instead of the short route.

I was pretty ill at the time. I was paranoid and fearful of most people. I thought that we were being mistreated everywhere we went because people were evil. I thought Angela and I had to rectify our situation by speaking to someone in authority. We paid for a room in a hotel off Bank Street, the main street that went through the downtown area of Ottawa.

"Angela," I said, "I really know a good restaurant around the corner. I'll go and get us some food."

Angela said, "OK," but at that time, she was acting really weird and paranoid about my motives and was really unsatisfied and angry with me. I went to a little Lebanese restaurant around the corner from the YWCA. I brought back two beef and chicken Shawarma combo plates (shaved beef, shaved chicken, potatoes, and salad) and a couple of pops. Immediately, Angela spat out her food and accused me of trying to poison her. She said, "Dave, you put powder on my food."

"What are you talking about?" I asked.

"There is white powder on my food." Angela thought I collaborated with the evil restaurant to poison her purposely (halluincation and persecutory delusion).

We slept throughout the night, and in the morning, Angela told me, "David, you better go to the hospital and check yourself in because you are sick."

I walked for an hour to Queensway-Carleton Hospital, near Carleton University. I waited a little while to see a nurse, and during the intake interview she said to me, "You are not feeling well."

I said, "That is right."

She then asked me, "What is your home address?"

"I don't have one."

I was then transferred to an examination room to be examined by a doctor. I had with me all my belongings—mostly clothes—in a tennis bag. The doctor came in, and I said, "I am not feeling too well."

He then left for a couple of minutes. When he came back, he said, "You are on crack; you are a druggie,"

Immediately, I told him in an offended tone, "No, I am not on crack; no, I am not a druggie."

The doctor left the room, and moments later, two security officers came into the room and escorted me off the property.

At that time, I had nowhere to go, so I walked back to the YWCA in the cold. By that time, Angela had left, and I did not know where she was or if she was ever coming back. I waited patiently in the hotel's waiting area, where there were many tables and chairs. After waiting for a couple of hours, I noticed two or three ambulances with blaring rotating orange lights that were shining from outside the entrance. At that time, I thought that this meant that the devils had caught up to us and that the area was dense with evil people. I thought that the ambulance lights were warning the evildoers in a threatening way that if they didn't behave themselves, God could instantly snuff out their lives.

Then, Angela placed a call from wherever she was to the YWCA front reception desk. I talked to her, and she told me, "Dave, I'll be back real soon."

It took her a couple of hours after that phone call to finally arrive at the hotel. I was concerned about our situation because I thought that Angela would have no way to actually have the opportunity to speak with the prime minister (grandiose delusion).

We were reunited, but we did not have any money to go back home to Toronto. We continually called my mom to ask her to wire us some money, but there was no answer. After we finally contacted her, she agreed to wire us some money to Ottawa. We ended up walking to the Money Mart by Parliament Hill and took a cab to the bus terminal, and then we took a late evening bus to Toronto.

CHAPTER 8

METRO EAST DETENTION CENTRE

In Toronto, we decided to take a cab to Kingston Road and finally found a motel that had a vacancy. This motel room was disgusting and filthy, so there was no way Angela was going to stay there. She took off with my winter coat during late that night. I was so tired and exhausted that I slept in the motel room anyway. I knew at that moment that Angela had left me for good. I had lost the power and purpose of being with Angela and I was really scared about being alone. I was forced to face myself and the fact that my paranoia might not be real.

The next morning, I left the motel with no inclination as to where to go. I decided that if Angela had left me, I might as well go to my mother's apartment. That was the last place I wanted to go, but I felt that I was a failure because Angela had rejected me, so I took my chances. I arrived at my mother's place in the afternoon, and my mother and brother took me in.

My mother suggested to me on many occasions that I visit the hospital. I never took her up on her offer, so one day my mother called a mental health crisis team to come to her apartment. When they arrived, I locked myself in the bathroom the whole time and ignored their requests to unlock the door. My family was trying to get me help, but I thought they were trying to weaken the world's holy spiritual powers, which rested solely on my shoulders, by placing me in a mental ward. I reasoned with myself that if I thwarted the execution of their evil schemes—because I thought there was nothing wrong with me—my holy presence would not be interrupted but rather increased (grandiose delusion).

My brother had decided to take his planned vacation to Scotland, leaving me behind with my mother. Since my brother was gone, I decided to take my brother's Honda Prelude for a spin. My destination was the nearest Wal-Mart. On my way, there was a car tailgating me very closely, which I did not appreciate. I stopped my brother's car and got out of the vehicle to pretend that something was wrong with it. I did this to impede the traffic because I felt that I was being pushed around in Toronto.

A police car happened to be doing a left turn into my lane, and it pulled right behind me to see what was going on. The officer watched me walk to the front of the vehicle and back to the driver's seat and drive away. As I drove away from my little drama scene, the officer followed me to the entrance of a shopping mall. Realizing that I was being followed, I did a U-turn at the entrance of the parking lot and sped in the opposite direction of where I'd come from. The cop put on his sirens and chased me down the road. I decided to stop my brother's car on the road, and that is when the police officer came out of his cruiser very aggressively. He tried to break the passenger window with his hands as it was rolled down a crack. I pulled into another parking lot, and that is when backup arrived on scene. Two police cruisers were now trying to block me in the parking lot. I escaped and raced down the road at 140 kph, doing one right turn and then another, and I lost the cops. I parked the car for a while on a quiet street and abandoned the car. Then I took a bus south and then north, and then I hopped back in the car and went back to my mother's place. When I arrived at the apartment after my expedition, I noticed that the digital telephone's message light was on. There was a message from the police officer who had tried to break my window for me to turn myself in. I ended up getting the password for the answering machine by pressing redial on the phone, and I erased the message. Later in the week, this same police officer got ahold of my mom, and she told the cop I was sick. Thankfully, the officer decided not to pursue the matter any further.

The next day, I noticed a Bell Telephone truck repairing the phone terminal panel outside. Immediately, I warned my mother to be on her best behavior because the Federal Bureau of Investigation (FBI) was watching me through satellite. I thought that the Bell technician was actually an FBI agent who was concerned about me (delusions: grandiose and ideas of reference).

That night, while my mom was out, I took some of her belongings, including her black witchy leather coat, and threw them into a nearby river. My rationale for throwing out her witchy-looking clothes was that doing so would reduce her evil power. I then ripped up her wedding photos and flushed them down the toilet. The next day, my mom discovered what I had done and called the police on me. I decided to take a shower; if the cops were going to take me into custody, they would have to do it when I was naked. The cops came and were ready to throw me out wet and naked, but my mom changed her mind, which angered them.

While staying at my mom's apartment, I noticed a Halloween costume that included a red and black plastic pitchfork and a devil mask with horns. My grandfather's WWI rifle was in the closet as well. I thought the costume in the closet confirmed that my mother and brother must be evil. The gun, on the other hand, did not have any evil connotations, but I did not feel comfortable with a rifle in the closet. I decided to call the police to inform them that there was a rifle in the apartment.

The police arrived within a few minutes. My brother tried to explain to them that I was mentally ill and that I was the person who had called. My brother tried to explain that the rifle was inoperative and was an artifact. The police officers were not convinced by my brother's story and asked for the rifle to be surrendered to them. My plan to release myself from the burden of always being the focus of wrongdoing seemed to be working. I wanted my mother and brother to be on the defense this time, instead of me always having the police called on me.

I knew that the police's attention would be redirected back to me in due time, so I ran out of the apartment complex and hid in the backyard, lying down in the wet snow in the dark winter night. I stayed there for eight minutes undetected, until my intuition told me that they would soon find me there. I moved back into the apartment building, sneaking my way into the basement laundry room of the building and hiding there until the police officers left. After the police left, I tried to get back into my mother's apartment, but she would not let me in. I slept in the hallway for a couple of nights until finally she let me in.

After being in the apartment for a few more days, I cornered my mom in her kitchen and confronted her about why she treated me the way she did when I was growing up. My mother did not respond to my questions, but I thought I was entitled to answers. She would not acknowledge to me that she was responsible for emotionally abusing me as a child. When she did not acknowledge any wrongdoing, that left me feeling invalidated, and it ticked me off.

In complete and utter disgust, I physically assaulted my mother. She left the apartment and went down to a neighbor's unit. After a few minutes, she came up to the apartment by herself, but I would not let her in. Not long after, I looked out the bathroom window. Standing in the parking lot was a Special Weapons and Tactics team (SWAT) member with a rifle in his arms. My mother must have called the cops and told them I had a gun. I know my mother is a hysterical woman and that under the circumstances she is capable of making up a lie to get attention, but give me a break. The SWAT team! Really?

I decided to leave the bathroom and shut the bathroom door behind me. I stayed in my brother's bedroom down the hallway. Then, a few minutes later, four big guys with big guns busted through the apartment door and stormed down the hallway toward the bathroom door. The SWAT members, realizing I had outsmarted them, as I was not in the bathroom, were none too pleased. Although I appeared calm, I was shaking inside, as my nerves were rattled beyond measure. When they entered the bedroom, they yelled at me, "Get on the ground!"

I just ignored their orders, and that is when the SWAT members threw me to the ground. They shackled me somewhat in my brother's room and finished their duties in the living room. They then took me out of the apartment in leg shackles and handcuffs. This ordeal was humiliating and painful; they carried me horizontally by these restraints to the police cruiser waiting outside. In the back of the cop car, I noticed someone hiding in the bushes with a camera to film me for the evening news.

The police officers transported me to the local police station, where I was placed in a cell for a couple of hours. Then I was transferred to the Metro East Detention Centre, where I ended up in a small cellblock with about five cells. The cellblock had a common room with a television and a contained shower unit. Everybody in the cellblock could view the television from inside their cells by looking through a Plexiglas window located on the doors of the cells. In the cellblock next to the television was a camera directed squarely at my cell. That way, my behavior could be observed through closed-circuit transmission. I was locked in my cell and never knew or cared if it was ever unlocked so I could enter the common area or have a shower.

I was ignored for a couple of days, until a social worker showed up outside my cell door offering her services. She said, "I can help you; I am a social worker."

I said, "Why the hell do I need a social worker in a place like this?"

The social worker came back a few times, and I just told her the same thing. During my entire stay at the centre, the television channel was on the Much Music station. I just wanted to watch a hockey game and declared my wishes to the rest of the inmates—but to no avail. On top of that, a bright light in my cell was lit twenty-four hours a day, making it very difficult to get any kind of sleep.

They sent a nurse who wanted to give me a shot, but I would not let her into my cell during the day, so she came late at night. I stayed up late at night so she would not be able to stick a needle in me when I was asleep. In the morning, four or five people came into my cell talking about something that I do not remember. Since I was scared of them, I went to the top bunk and hunkered down in a defensive position in the corner. Later in the day, a man knocked on my cell door.

I said, "Get lost."

He responded, "I am the warden of the jail."

Again, I said, "Get lost."

Five days passed without any human contact except the person distributing tea and food; he wanted to make small talk. The food there was terrible, so I refused to eat. On the fifth day, the warden and a guard came to my cell door and invited me to come outside my cell to receive a change of clothes.

I said, "I am content with the clothes I have on. No thank you." I splashed water from the metal sink all over the concrete cell floor and placed my mattress against the cell door, barricading myself in the cell.

The warden and jail guard, who had realized they could not trick me to come out of my cell, said, "You have to attend morning court."

I ignored their request and continued with my protest until two jail guards stormed my cell to tackle me. The first guard slipped on the floor as I just looked at him; the second guard got ahold of me. The guards then bound me with leg shackles and handcuffs. They took me to a room downstairs to be chained to another prisoner and then transferred into the back of a prisoner van.

At the courthouse, I was stored by myself in a holding cell in the basement, where all the cells were located, for four hours. They then took me up to court and were rough with me, which I did not appreciate. In the prisoner's box, I sat when they told me to stand, and when they told me to sit, I stood, telling them out loud that they were all a bunch of liars. My family attended and pleaded with the judge that I was mentally ill and needed help.

I was then put into my cell in the basement for two more hours, and that is when the judge and his colleagues came to observe my condition. The judge confirmed from that screening that I was unfit for trial. I stayed at the courthouse for yet another two hours, and all I had to eat and drink the whole time was a cheese sandwich and some coffee. Around 5:00 p.m., the guards took me out of the cell and transferred me to the prisoner van. Again, the guards were really rough with me, and again, I did not appreciate that. As the prisoner van door was about to close, I spat directly onto one of the guard's faces from a long distance. It was a direct hit. The door then closed, and I was safe.

I sat by myself in the prisoner van, as many prisoners were chained to each other in the back of the van. The courthouse sent me back to Metro East Detention Centre, where they transferred me to a different cell this time. In the mental health government clerk's office, there was paperwork for me to be transferred to a hospital, but they forget to bring it to court, so I was transferred back to jail.

This infuriated my father. He said, "Government workers can't do anything right the first time; it takes them a couple of times."

The mental health workers blamed the mistake on government cutbacks ordered by Mike Harris, our Ontario premier at the time.

I was then placed in a cell where freezing cold air blew into the room through the air vents. They were going to leave me in the room with no clothes, until I requested to have some clothes because it was freezing. A guard gave me an anti-suicide vest, through the door slot used for food trays. The vest is comparable to what you would be given at the dentist office when they are doing X-Rays on your teeth. It was made of a heavy material, so that an individual would not be able to rip it apart to hang oneself. I used the vest as a pillow and blanket to keep warm so that I could get some sleep. I curled in the fetal position by having my arms and legs scrunched inside the vest.

The next morning, I was taken to the Queen Street Mental Health Centre. As soon as I arrived, I became frightened of going in because I thought they wanted to euthanize me again. I refused to exit the prisoner van. When the guards were about to use force, I volunteered to walk to what I thought was my death.

PART 2

ON THE ROAD TO RECOVERY

QUEEN STREET MENTAL HEALTH CENTRE

I arrived at the Queen Street Mental Health Centre during the morning, and they needed to assess if I was fit to stand trial. The guards and staff at the centre took me to a room that was designated as a transition area and that was secluded from the ward on the same floor. I remember that I was very ill at that time, so I was huddled in the corner out of complete fear and paranoia. However, I somehow sensed that this was a safe haven and that I belonged at this place. I knew at that moment that I was where I should be and that everything was going to be OK.

Then my doctor entered the padded room, which reeked of urine, and approached me. A few staff members were behind him as he bowed down on his knees before me. At that moment, I thought it was about time somebody recognized me for my royal presence (grandiose delusion). I graciously listened to his compassionate words. A few minutes after the doctor left, ten staff entered my room, turned me on my back, pulled down my pants, and gave me a needle in my bum. Then later in the day, my clothes were taken from me, and they gave me an anti-suicide vest.

The next day, I was given a room at the end of a hallway; the room had a door with a window in it. Whenever people in the ward walked down that hallway, they looked into my room, and I felt a spiritual soreness around my abdomen area. When I walked down the hallway at nighttime, I remember feeling that the devil was chasing me and taunting me. That feeling was terrible. All I could feel was an extremely violent evil presence. I thought that because I did something good by being in a safe environment, the devil was ticked off because he had lost his grip on my life. I thought, *Wow, the devil has finally revealed himself to me*, and I did not like his true colors. The feeling was so raw that I felt awful for about a week.

A man next to my room claimed he was Jesus. I thought, *Wow, there can't be two of us who are Jesus*, so I took on a new identity: King David. I was feeling such enormous pressure from mental anguish about being attacked by the devil and my soreness that I ventured to this man's room for help. He told me to kneel, and he led a prayer to rescue me from my affliction. Surprisingly, I felt a lot better and was greatly relieved after praying with this man.

I asked for a room transfer although my pains had subsided. After a few days, my transfer request was granted, and I was transferred to a room that had four beds instead of the single room. On the first day I was transferred to the new room, I remember taking my new medication that was distributed by the nurse. The medication was so powerful that I could barely make it back to my room. I stumbled, leaning on the wall to hold me up and guide me.

The next day, my medication was changed or reduced, but the guy who claimed he was Jesus told me, "Do not take the medication." I followed his instruction, placing a ripped-up cloth in the back of my mouth to absorb the liquid antipsychotic medication. After a couple of days without medication in my system, I told one of the nurses that I was using a ripped-up cloth to absorb the medication. They changed my medication to pill form, and from then on, I started taking my medication, and that is when I started getting better.

In the ward, we were awakened at 7:00 a.m. for breakfast during the week; on the weekends, we could skip breakfast and sleep in. After breakfast, every patient on the ward slept until lunch. I couldn't go back to sleep, so I was basically the only person awake on the ward in between breakfast and lunch during the week. The food was great at the centre, and most of the meals we had there were equal to what a good hotel would serve.

In my new room, I met Jason, and I really liked him. We hung out most of the time, and he was the one who got me back into the habit of smoking cigarettes. I requested to have a room transfer because a guy in my room kept stealing cigarettes from me. I ended up in a single room situated beside the common smoking room. Since the smoking room door made a loud noise when patients or staff entered or exited the room, it was difficult to get any rest. In addition, a radio in the smoking room sounded muffled through the wall. I told this guy Chucky, "If 'Back at One' by Bryan McKnight comes on the radio, then come and get me." I then requested to be transferred to my old room, which had four beds in it. Thankfully, the guy who was stealing from me before was not on the ward anymore.

Because I was feeling better and recovering from my illness, I decided to spend my newfound energy running up and down the ward. That is when they started giving me Valium to relax my muscles. On Friday afternoons, we had outdoor play in the yard, and when I played volleyball, I could not figure out why I could not hit the ball over the net. It took me until a couple of years later to realize after that Valium was a muscle relaxant. As a result, I refrained from physical exercise and just watched TV. I was pretty upset with one guy on the ward because he hogged control of the TV, keeping it on the BET channel all the time. I heard the "Thong" song by Sisco about a million times and tried my best not to go crazy. I tried to change the channel to watch the hockey game, but that lasted only a few minutes, and I did not bother to challenge the TV hog.

A certain male nurse liked me, and as we lined up for breakfast, lunch, or dinner he put me at the front of the line for some reason. One night, this same nurse thought he was doing me a favor when he snuck in some Swiss Chalet chicken for me, but as far as I was concerned, the food at the centre was better than any restaurant. The patients on the ward had to enter into a locked dining hall to eat their meals. For the most part, my dining experiences were pleasant ones except for one time.

A new patient in our ward was always trying to intimidate the patients by his demeanor and by staring at them with a vicious look. One day, he sat at the next table beside mine and looked repeatedly over his shoulder at me. I said to him, "What are you looking at?"

He then poured his cup of apple juice all over my head. The staff went to Code Red and separated us. The staff surrounded me to protect me. Then they called security and took him back to jail.

In the ward was a guy who had robbed a bank because he broke up with his girlfriend. He played Collective Soul on the guitar in the dining hall for the patients, and I thought he was pretty cool. One day, all the patients were locked into the dining hall although it was not the proper time to eat. The staff quarantined the ward and dispatched security to enter the ward and remove this patient because he had threatened a nurse.

I put up a note on the ward's billboard; in it, I explained my close relationship with the Heavenly Father. I also slipped a similar note under the door of a meeting room where my two psychiatrists were collaborating. The next day, I was invited to a room where the doctors and staff interviewed me. The room was completely silent. I asked, "Can you hear the silence?" but they just looked at me funny.

The next day, a psychiatrist in training, under the supervision of my doctor, interviewed me, and he asked if I had smoked marijuana. I told him that I did not inhale, and my doctor got a good laugh out of it. The staff at Queen Street Mental Health Centre really took care of me during my three months there, and I was fit for court. I had two psychiatrists at the centre, and the female one asked me one day, "What can I do for you, David?"

I said, "You can spend more time with me." I never spent much time with my psychiatrists, although I needed their help. I gradually began to enter reality, as my medication began doing its work. It was a very scary experience to realize that I was not Jesus or King David and that the whole mission with Angela had no purpose. When I lost my grandiose sense of self, it was depressing and disappointing to understand that I was a person with little significance in the world. It was frightening and overwhelming that there was a vast world out there beyond what I could figure out at the time.

At the centre, the social worker arranged for me to live in a group home in the Parkdale area of Toronto, which was close to the centre. The judge at the courthouse ruled that I was not responsible for my actions because I was not in my right mind. The charges were dropped, and I was released on three years' probation. My dad and brother picked me up after court and took me to Swiss Chalet near the courthouse. Then we went to the group home where I would be living.

When we first went to register for the group home, a polite fellow greeted us. My father thought this gentleman was the doctor of the home, so my dad talked to him openly about me. My dad found out later that the person in charge of admissions was actually a mental patient (although my brother and I already knew this at the time). The home was an older big house with a television lounge in the entrance. The mental patients in the home watched the Weather Channel for most of their waking hours, and again I thought, *What does a guy have to do to watch a hockey game?*

The minute I entered the home, I wanted to get the heck out of there. Most of the people there were really sick, and clearly I did not belong there. I was awakened at 3:00 a.m. by a man who could not walk but had to pee during the night. When this gentleman woke up during the night, he fell out of his bed and crashed onto the floor, making a loud banging noise. To get to the washroom, he smacked his walker on the ground as he dragged his body along the floor. I called my brother from the home about ten times a day because I was scared and full of anxiety. I was now in the free world, not confined for three months as I had been before. I now see why criminals reoffend when they are released from prison or jail: Being outside in the world without the routine, the safety, and the security they had once in an institution is an overwhelming, frightening experience. There were so many options and opportunities now available to me that I did not know which way to turn. This created a lot of anxiety and fear because I felt vulnerable and incapable to adapt to my new circumstances. It is like throwing a house cat into the jungle to fend for itself.

At the home, I contacted my friend Sydney and his wife, who lived in Toronto. They told me to visit them, but I think they were shocked about what had happened to me and my health. When I realized that the conditions of my release allowed me to visit my dad as much as I wanted, I told him, "I want to live with you."

I immediately moved in with my dad. He lived in a small town ninety minutes north of Toronto.

CHAPTER 10

LIVING IN LINDSAY

I arrived in Lindsay in Spring 2000. Lindsay was a quiet town with not much going on, but at least I had a stable place to live. My dad's apartment was above The Grand Hotel, located on the main street of town. This hotel was home to a popular family restaurant and bar. During my first week in Lindsay, my dad and I adopted a female tuxedo cat, and we named her April. I spent about one week in my dad's one bedroom apartment, and then I moved across the hallway to a larger two-bedroom unit. After I moved into the new apartment, my dad, brother, and I went to the storage facility in Toronto to get the rest of my belongings. All that remained were a couch, a bed, a desk, and some clothes that did not fit me very well.

I felt so ashamed about having Paranoid Schizophrenia that I could not face the friends I had. It did not matter anyhow, because they did not bother with me when they found out I was sick and away from them. The only person who tried to contact me, I learned later, was my ex-girlfriend, but my family buffered her out of my life and told her I was unavailable for her. I felt I had lost everything, and this feeling of devastation suffocated me. The heaviness of this burden was almost too much to bear. I cried out to the Lord, "Oh, My God!" as I punched myself in the arm. I then raised my fist at the sky, and I said to the Lord, "It is going to take me ten years to get out of this mess." I put my middle finger to the heavens above and defiantly told God, "This is all you got; bring it on." I realized that I had hit rock bottom. It made me feel very sad and disappointed, but I knew I had to accept my life situation no matter how difficult it was. I figured the only thing I could do was to move on and try to get my life and health back in order, but it was a bitter pill to swallow.

During this time, my dad did not know that I lacked the appetite that was required to eat his large healthy meals. He got angry if I did not eat all the food on my plate, so I forced it down. The main side effect of my antipsychotic medication, called Risperidal or Risperidone, is weight gain. It didn't take me long to go from 250 lbs to 300 lbs. The weight gain was so dramatic that I would bump into furniture because I was not used to maneuvering a big body around. In addition to being a large fellow now, I was very sick.

For example, I went to the Welfare Office to apply for government support until my Ontario Disability Support Program application was approved. When I was there, the clerks in the office did not even question my application. I was pacing up and down the office corridor, making the staff in the building nervous. It was more than anxiety; I basically suffered from continuous panic attacks. I felt that the world was ending, but it wasn't. The panic attacks subsided through time and turned into anxiety that I could cope with by smoking cigarettes. In addition to the anxiety, I lacked motivation and was easily overwhelmed. I became easily stressed and feared having to do the simplest things in life. I was also so paranoid about people and their motives that I rarely strayed from the confines of the household. I thought that everybody was watching me, which they probably were, because I was living in a small town.

One day, I decided to go to the store to buy some cigarettes. The lady downstairs, who ran the dollar store below, was outside having a cigarette when I came back. She intrusively asked me, "Where did you go, David?" At that moment, I realized I had just been indoctrinated into small-town life.

I was so upset that I'd lost my freedom to do what I pleased without being under the watchful eye of others that I called my mom and told her, "Get me the heck out of this place."

My mother did not respond to my request, as she was in no position to help me or did not care.

My dad met an older woman, Millie, when he first moved into town. They met at the local dance that took place at the Armories. She used to have a huge crush on him, but he just wanted to remain friends. Millie was young at heart and on a moment's notice would go anywhere or do just about anything. Some people in Millie's building were jealous that she was so vibrant and hanging out with my dad. One night, she came home and found a note on her door. The note said, "Millie, your parking spot number, is 42 not your age."

Since I did not have any friends to hang out with, I was pretty bored with life. Millie invited my dad to the movies, and he asked me if I wanted to tag along. The movie, "Something's Gotta Give," starred Jack Nicolson and Diane Keaton. In the movie, Jack's character was an older fellow who was going out with a young girl, Diane Keaton's daughter. Jack was unsatisfied about being with a younger woman because they had nothing in common. Diane convinced Jack to go out with her because they had more in common, although Jack did not want to. The moral of this story is that my dad should have ignored younger women and gone out with Millie because they had more in common. Millie was 77 at the time, and my dad was 62. The funniest thing is that I had to explain to my dad what his friend Millie was trying to tell him. My dad had no clue; it was funny.

Not long after my dad got the two-bedroom apartment, my brother moved in with us. He had quit his low-paying job at a soft drink corporation in Toronto. At the time, I yearned for the glory days when I had attended university. To try to get back into good mental shape—and to satisfy my need to do something—I enrolled in a creative writing class at Fleming College in Peterborough. Peterborough was a forty-five-minute drive from Lindsay, and my dad and brother would sometimes take me there. My dad would hang out in Peterborough while I attended my three-hour class, which lasted fifteen weeks. I thought that taking a creative writing course would help with my writing skills for my book.

When the creative writing class was over, all I had in my life was working out at the local gym, shooting pool at the Grand, and visiting Tim Horton's with my brother. Later on, I tried to get into Trent University, but Trent sent me a letter to respond by a certain date for my application, but I got the letter after that date, so it was too late. It was a good thing that the letter arrived late, because Schizophrenia had a good grip on me. My thoughts were scattered, and not connected with each other, as they ran rampat in my mind. It was taxing to do even the simpliest of tasks, because I was easily overwhelmed. It did not help that I was fearful for no reason, and I lacked motivation. I was not really in any shape to be taking university courses.

It was difficult for three of us to live in a two-bedroom apartment together, and my brother had to sleep on the couch. We all became dissatisfied with our close quarters. For example, my brother would fall asleep with the television on, the sound blasting all night. This upset my father, as my brother seemed to be inconsiderate of our need to sleep in tranquility. My father asked him, "Why don't you shut off the TV when you go to bed?"

My brother replied, "Why didn't you shut it off when you were up?"

There was so much tension between my father and brother that they made a bet. My brother said, "I will quit smoking, Dad, if you quit drinking." My brother eventually lost that bet, but they did quit their bad habits for a couple of months. When my dad took up drinking again, he sneaked back into the habit quietly. My dad would go to the liquor store and purchase Alpinebitter and then later Dr. McGillicuddy's cinnamon schnapps. According to my dad, Alpinebitter was not actually alcohol because it was made from herbs and spices; in addition, he thought we could be fooled by the fact that the schnapps had a "Doctor" label on the bottle.

My dad needed a break from my brother because he was not free to drink anymore, so he sent me instead to spend Christmas with my Aunt Frances at her son's home in Maple Ridge, British Columbia. At the time, I was still getting used to my medication and the effects of my illness. I slept a lot during my visit, but I did find the strength to visit Whistler with my cousin Ryan, who came on the trip.

When I returned from this vacation in the new year, my dad and I began hunting for a house to purchase in town. Within a month, we found and purchased a home, but the possession date was not until three months later. A month after buying the house, we gave our two months' notice to vacate the apartment unit. In the meantime, I convinced my dad to let my brother buy me a puppy because we were going to move into a house. It was difficult living with a dog in the apartment, but we made due. We moved into the house at the end of summer, and Calvin was excited to finally have a backyard to run around and play in.

I had a dog for company, but I needed something more than animal companionship. I was so desperate for friendship that I even tried to be-

friend the convenience store clerk. I usually went to the store to buy cigarettes, and one day I told her, "I am writing a book."

She said, "I would love to read your book, David."

I told her in advance what the book was about, but she still wanted to
read it anyway. I gave her a copy and she read the rough draft. Whenever
I went into the store after that, though, she looked at me with disgust and
fear. I told this story to my dad, and he suggested I sign up for the Canadian
Mental Health Association (CMHA) so that I could meet some people. I
took his advice to heart, and that was a good thing because being involved
with CMHA, I met a lot of people who had the same life circumstances as
mine.

When I first became involved with CMHA in 2002, I volunteered as a
receptionist for the front desk of the office. One day while volunteering, I
went into the lunchroom to eat. I told Janice, a social worker there about a
man I knew who was also a social worker there: "I think Dan is going to get
a divorce because he is never home and is neglecting his family."

Janice said, "I am his wife."

Right then and there, I realized that I had made a mistake. It was em-
barrassing to be caught red handed as a gossiper in this small town, but I
was just trying to fit in. Later on, I became involved in the social recreation
program. We went for walks, played floor hockey, played baseball, did arts
and crafts, and played games.

That summer of 2004, a CMHA barbecue was held at Janice's parents'
place, and I met a guy named Kevin. He gave me his phone number, and
I was so excited to finally have a friend after all these years. Pretty soon,

Kevin and I were hanging out almost every day. We rode our bicycles through town and visited the local fast food restaurants. After a couple of weeks, though, I saw less of Kevin because he started hanging around a girl that lived close to his apartment building. He did not find her attractive, but she had attractive friends.

One day, I went to this girl's house (I had never met her before), and she pulled my pants around my waist out and then put a bunch of ice cubes down my pants. I thought, *What the heck is going on here? I don't even know this girl.* She had four children who had four different fathers, and I remember that her youngest girl was an infant because she was being neglected, and this upset me. This infant had to pick up the bottle to feed herself—all by herself—while sitting in a car seat on the floor in the house. I said to myself, "I can't handle seeing this; I must never come back here."

Then through this girl, Kevin met a girl named Crystal, who had four daughters. Kevin had sex with her, and she asked me one day, "Are you gay, David?"

I answered, "No, I am not gay," but I was not about to sleep with someone who had slept with the whole town. At Crystal's house, about six people were all having sex with each other even though they were married. The girls were having babies from all kinds of different guys. I thought, *This is like I am on a "Jerry Springer" episode!* I thought, *I can't handle this. I have to find some new friends.*

Janice then hooked me up with Melissa, who had recently moved to town from the States, where she'd been living with her ex-husband. I thought to myself, *Finally, I am going to meet my soul mate after all these years.* While I was friends with Melissa, I landed a volunteer job at a computer store. First, my dad asked my social worker, "Is it OK for someone with Schizophrenia to drive a car?"

My social worker said, "It is safe for David to drive a vehicle."

Then, after receiving that confirmation, my dad let me start using the car, so I could go to work. I cleaned the shelves and helped the computer technicians update software on the computers that came into the store. Many of these computers were loaded with spyware, so we had to clean up these infections.

After getting a month's experience at the computer store, I landed a volunteer job at Staples. I organized the stock in the store and handled customer inquiries. It was tough on me to get up at 7:00 a.m. every morning to be in for work at 9:00 a.m., and I worked until 1:00 p.m. four days a week. My nurse was proud that I was working, and I was brimming with confidence because of it. Although there was an upside to being employed, I still quit at the end of my six-week term and did not pursue paid employment because the stress was too much for me to handle.

Melissa read in the local newspaper that Kevin was trying to lure young girls to Toronto. I knew Kevin was charming, but he was also big trouble, and the police told everybody in town through the local newspaper that there was nothing to be concerned about, but I begged to differ. A few years earlier, Kevin had sold roses at the nightclubs in Toronto, and he always talked to me about his yearning for the old days.

While I was friends with Melissa, I met a friend named Russell at another CMHA barbecue that took place at one of their group homes in town. Russell could read lips, and he could speak very well despite being deaf. My brother bought me a fax machine so Russell could communicate with me, and he faxed me when he wanted to go out for coffee. Everything was going well between us until I freaked him out one day because I was having an episode. I told Russell, "I am a general in an army."

That was enough for Russell to abandon me as a friend. The stress from quitting smoking for three months must have triggered an episode. Our relationship was cut short, and that was too bad because I really liked Russell. Melissa and I hung out together for a couple of months until I realized I could not handle her mood swings. Melissa was bipolar and would invite me to her place to do something; then, when I arrived at her home 30 minutes later, she became suicidal. Melissa was moody and it was a cold winter, with average temperatures being – 25 degrees celsius, so I chose not to go outside to visit her, and I allowed our relationship to dwindle.

Every Saturday afternoon, my dad and I went to the local Royal Canadian Legion to attend the meat roll, where we would buy tickets to win meat and to have a few drinks. We quickly earned a reputation of being real winners at the legion because we were so lucky on the meat roll. One day when we went to legion they had four specials on which you could win. Would you believe that we won three specials out of four? After we won that day, whenever we came back to the legion, the members taunted us in a joking manner, "There are the winners!"

We felt like celebrities, but who wouldn't with the kind of patrons the legion attracted? I remember going to the legion one afternoon, and a guy we knew had on jogging pants and a shirt he must have been wearing for a month. Well, when this guy went up to purchase a meat ticket, all you could see were fecal stains on the back of his pants. When nobody in the legion was disgusted by this repulsive sight, I realized that I'd have to move out of this town.

The town had no class, and they only accepted people who were originally from there. We tried to accommodate the locals, but the more we tried, the more they ignored us. Most people just wanted to know your business and never really bothered with us. When my dad purchased the home in town, most of the people he used to hang around with stopped visiting us because they were jealous. Many women tried to attract my dad as a partner, but my dad was not interested in them because they were not his type. I found it difficult to have any intelligent conversation with anybody. That left me very lonely and feeling socially deprived. I had a deep hunger to relate to anything other than the stupidity and ignorance of the town. I think the aura of the town was rubbing off on my dad. One day, I said to him, "Let's go out to McDonald's for something to eat."

He told me, "David, we are not millionaires."

Then, it was a Friday night and I wanted to do something. My dad said, "David, clean the toilets."

Then one morning, my dad was having a big argument with someone in the house. I thought, *Oh my God! Dad has a woman over, and he is arguing with her.*

All I heard was my father calling the woman derogatory names. When I went downstairs to investigate, I found out that he was arguing with the cat. April wanted tuna early in the morning, and she was meowing at my dad to hurry up and open the can of tuna.

All of these events buried me emotionally; I felt hopeless with no way of escape, until one day, Sue, a social worker at CMHA, lent me some Christian music CDs and books. After reading about 15 books and listening to 10 CDs, I went out and bought a book of my own: *The Purpose Driven Life*, by Rick Warren. The book says, "Listen: God put you where you are for a purpose! He has every hair on your head numbered, and he knows your address. You had better stay put until he chooses to move you." p. 263. And "God often attaches a major weakness to a major strength to keep our egos in check. A limitation can act as a governor to keep us from going too fast and running ahead of God." p. 274.

My dad and I used to have parties in our basement, but we were the only ones there. We would drink beer and listen to music from my music collection. We would talk about how dissatisfied we were with the people in town because they were not meeting our needs. All we asked was for somebody to spend time with us and talk with us. That was obviously too much to ask because most people in town could not or did not want to relate to us. We just did not fit in the town, and eventually our status got downgraded because we were so dissatisfied with the town.

Although the town was no good, we tried to make the best of where we were. After my dad finished ice fishing with his friend Wayne, who was Millie's son-in-law, we decided to begin a new health regimen to get out of our social-deprivation rut. We both quit drinking, and we both went on a diet. It was winter, and we walked three hours a day just to have something to do and to get into shape. After a few months, we were both feeling better and looking good as well. We both lost weight; I dropped from 300 lbs to about 265 lbs.

We then decided to pay a summer's visit to my brother for two weeks in Moncton, New Brunswick. After working for a year in Toronto, my brother had been transferred to the East Coast. He had already been in Moncton for a year and had purchased a beautiful four-bedroom home there. While in Moncton, we checked out the city and visited Prince Edward Island, where we enjoyed lobster and French fries. It was a good time, and it was nice to get away from the mundane life we had in Lindsay.

When I came back from our trip, Angela called me out of the blue, and I talked to her for the first time in many years. I agreed to meet with her at the Yonge and Eglinton Tim Horton's in Toronto. We met the next week, and I got closure over our relationship, even though she wanted to start something new.

My dad wanted to sell our dog Calvin, so he put an advertisement in the paper. One summer evening, a couple from Norland came over to look at Calvin. I was nervous because I really wanted to sell Calvin, and all the other prospective buyers who had seen Calvin passed up the opportunity of having him because he was too hyperactive. The couple seemed to be really interested in Calvin because he was the kind of dog they were looking for, and they were not afraid to pay our reasonable asking price. We were not giving Calvin away for nothing because we had paid a good price for him, and we had spent money on him. We had taken Calvin to the veterinarian to get his shots and to get fixed.

All of us were at the kitchen table making small talk about Calvin, and then we agreed it would be nice to see Calvin run and play in the backyard. The couple had brought their two children with them, and in the backyard, rambunctious Calvin roughly knocked over the little girl and then the little boy. I thought, *Oh no, that is not good; they are never going to buy Calvin now.* But, both parents started laughing, and the mother said, "Isn't that cute."

I thought to myself, *Really?*

Anyhow, they bought Calvin, who was full of energy and who needed a big place to live where he could run around. The couple from Norland had some property with a pond, and we were happy to sell Calvin to someone who really wanted him and who would look after him in the manner he needed.

During my time in Lindsay, I received very little treatment with how to cope with Schizophrenia except medication. I was on a medication called Cogentin, in addition to the antipsychotic medication I was taking religiously. Cogentin was used to reduce tremors in the body. I do not know why I was on Cogentin because Risperidal is a newer antipsychotic known not to cause tremors. I never had tremors of the body, but I did have anxiety, and maybe the two got confused. Cogentin made me sleep a lot, and as a result, I was very drowsy throughout the day. Cogentin also blurred my vision.

My nurse in Lindsay recognized early on that I should not be taking Cogentin. She told me, "David, you should stop taking Cogentin."

I then tried to quit taking it, but I told my nurse, "I feel extremely sick when I stop taking Cogentin."

She kept me on Cogentin for six years. In the sixth year, my psychiatrist finally spoke to me about getting off this medication: "David, I think you should stop taking Cogentin."

I told the psychiatrist, "I feel sick when I stop taking Cogentin."

He said, "David, you will feel terrible for about a week, but then you will be OK."

I wish my nurse had told me that six years earlier, but she had not. I saw my psychiatrist only every six months. I never really got to know my psychiatrists because there was a new psychiatrist every year, and they never spent any real quality time with me. Lindsay was just an outreach clinic for the Whitby Mental Health Centre, and that is why my nurse thought she was a doctor; she was in charge while the psychiatrists were away.

The next day, I was off Cogentin, and I remember being in the backyard because it was autumn. I remember that for the first time in six years, I could hear the sound of the leaves on the trees blowing in the wind and the birds singing. Eckhart Tolle, a popular spiritual leader, has written many books about how your mind works and about the spiritual side of life. At this time, I discovered my pain body, which Eckhart Tolle talked about. The pain body is a negative trapped energy field that causes soreness around the abdomen area. I was not reading or listening to Eckhart Tolle then, but I do remember the pain that I could not explain at the time.

My dad asked me, "David, do you want to move?"

I said, "If we don't move, I will just live in my bedroom doing nothing."

From that moment on, my dad realized that if we didn't move then, our life would never change for the better.

The next day, my dad had the real estate company come to the house and put a sign on the lawn. My dad's friend Wayne looked at the sign on the lawn and pretended that nothing was going on. The people in Lindsay had us at the bottom of the social hierarchy, and we were glad that the house sold in three weeks. We then visited towns where we might want to live. We checked out London, Barrie, and Brantford, but we did not feel at home in any of those towns.

We went with our first choice, Peterborough. The night before the moving truck was to arrive in the morning, my dad almost burnt down the house. He had put all the pots and pans away in a box but wanted to cook spaghetti. He took a plastic bowl that looked like a metal bowl and put in on the burner.

I told him, "Dad, that bowl is plastic."

"Shut up," he said.

Then before you knew it, the bowl caught on fire, almost burning down the house.

It was time to move on, and after being in rut for so many years, I was glad my dad had the courage to move to a new town.

CHAPTER 11

LIVING IN PETERBOROUGH

We arrived in Peterborough in September 2006. We rented a two-bedroom apartment in the east end of town. Our apartment building was very close to the Memorial Center, home of the Ontario Hockey League's Peterborough Pete's. It was a busy end of town, and I remember being captivated and overwhelmed by the amount of traffic and people. I realized that it would take some time and effort to adjust to my new surroundings and way of life, so I decided to take an Introduction to French class at the local college.

One time before I went to French class, my father cooked an unforgettable meal for me. This dinner consisted of sausages, beans, cabbage, and sauerkraut. I told my dad, "I can't eat that before going to French class."

My dad replied, "Shut up, David; don't be a wimp."

Of course you can imagine what happened next, but with strict discipline I thwarted the irrupting gas explosion invasion for three hours.

In French class, I met a pretty cool guy named Daniel. One day, he invited me and another guy to a sports bar to watch a hockey game. I got so excited that Daniel and the other classmate looked at me, likely thinking, *What is wrong with this guy?* I was starving for friendship and desperate to interact with anybody who was at least normal.

I never got around to watching the hockey game with Daniel, but the feeling that somebody wanted to spend time with me gave me hope. I earned a B+ average in my Introduction to French class at Fleming College, and the following semester in January, I decided to enroll in the intermediate French class. I attended only a couple of classes and dropped out because I was getting sick. I was aware that I may be coming down with a mild episode, because my mind was overburdened with incessant fearful thoughts. To the best of my abilities I ignored those thoughts, and in a short time they went away. The transition of moving to a new town to start a new life all over again was stressful and a culture shock to me.

At the time, my father controlled every aspect of my life. I was slowly recovering from Schizophrenia and needed to be cared for, but my Father controlled my life to the extreme. I tried to exert some independence from him, but it was very difficult because I was used to being so dependent upon him. I sensed that my father saw my desire to be more independent as being a direct threat to his self-esteem, so that is why he insulted me when I wanted to express my own individuality.

My self-esteem was also negatively influenced by the fact that I did not have control over my feelings; I was subjugated to riding the emotional rollercoaster of my father's moods. I never knew what would trigger his anger because his moods were unpredictable. This left me very unstable because I always had to walk on eggshells to keep the peace. There was not much

I could do at the time because I was vulnerable and dependent upon my father for my basic needs.

One day, I decided that I had had enough. I was going to push back and create some space for myself, but I did not know how. When attacking me emotionally, my father accused me and blamed me for perceived mishaps or misfortunes. When I defended my innocent position, my father would find the solution to his problem, which nullified the existence of his blame. These emotional tirades were recycling for years but not as intensely as they were at this time.

Dr. Adrian Rogers came onto the television and gave me some advice: "When the devil attacks you just 'Praise the Lord.'" That is exactly what I did. When my dad came home drunk and angry from the bar, I would say, "Praise the Lord" over and over again until my dad became disoriented and confused. From that moment on, the enemy who was against me became identified and clear. It took a couple of weeks for me finally to get the courage to confront my father about his behavior. I told him, "You are the devil." I proceeded to spit in his face and left the apartment. I then took an evening bus to Toronto to live with my mother.

My mother accepted me at her apartment, but she was surprised I had left my father to live with her without giving her any warning. My mother lived in a seniors' apartment on Yonge Street. It was difficult to sleep there because of the traffic noise and sirens from emergency vehicles coming and going late at night. While living with my mother, I applied to Peterborough Housing to get a subsidized apartment. To get ahead on the list, I decided to claim that my living arrangements were abusive.

The time I spent living with my mother went pretty well. She was desperate for company, and I assisted her with living costs. It was a strange living situation because my mother had been emotionally abusive to me in the past, and now we were forced to get along. My mother's apartment was a se-niors' building that did not allow non-seniors to live there. Some residents in the building were becoming suspicious that I might be living with my mother. After living with her for six months, from February to July 2007, I found out that it would take more than a year to get a subsidized apartment in Peterborough. My dad had met a nice woman named Nancy and had bought a house in the west end of Peterborough. For these two reasons, I decided to take them up on their invitation to live with them.

I did not know what to expect from my father, but I was hoping that my dad was on his best behavior because he was with Nancy. My assumption was right, and Nancy was a really nice lady—and that made my transition to my new life that much easier. I had my own little apartment without a kitchen in the basement of the house. However, the area we lived in was not very friendly. I didn't seem to be able to connect with anybody my age in the neighborhood. I needed some type of friendship, so my dad once again hooked me up with CMHA, which organizes social and recreation activities.

Peter, a social worker from CMHA, called my cell phone and invited me to come out to play volleyball. We played volleyball every Thursday at the YMCA in Peterborough. I met a lot of people there but nobody I could really go out with or be close friends with.

In the summer, I said to Nancy, "I would like to take part-time psychology courses at Trent University."

Nancy immediately said, "Go for it, David; you can do it."

Although my dad was a bit skeptical and reserved his judgment, I enrolled in the psychology program at Trent University and got accepted before the fall term began.

My first day at Trent was nerve racking. I had been out of the university scene for almost six years. It took me a lot of courage to walk into the auditorium where my Introduction to Psychology class was to be held. I became shocked when I realized that the auditorium held about 400 people and that it was full—and that about 95 percent of those people were young, beautiful girls under the age of 20. I thought to myself, *I do not belong here! What am I doing here? I must be crazy.*

I ignored my chattering mind and ended up getting a B average in that class. There, I learned the fundamentals of psychology, which I would need for the rest of my upper-level courses. I learned how to write a psychology paper and how to take a multiple choice psychology exam.

While I was attending my first year of university, Nancy and Dad went to Las Vegas, leaving me alone to house sit with the dog and cat. Nancy had a beautiful Belgian sheepdog named Lady. Now, April, my cat, had to learn to live with a new dog, which was not rambunctious like Calvin. April eventually became best friends with Lady, and they hung out together most of the time. Once when I was in the bathroom, I opened the door to find that Lady had sent April down the hallway to check up on me. The more April and Lady lived together, the more April began acting like a dog.

It was summer time, and I enrolled in a course that I needed in order to fulfill my program requirements. Research Statistics for Psychology was one of the most difficult courses that psychology students have trouble with. The course took place in a room smaller than the big auditorium. It took some time for me to get used to this new personal environment, where you had to interact with people. In the class was a blonde girl I liked. She sat

right beside me. I suspected she liked me because she would text message a girl above our row after I just talked to her, and that made me nervous. Many girls in class liked me, and I found it difficult to concentrate on the lecture. One girl, down below in the pit of the classroom, would throw her hair up in the air whenever I looked in her direction.

The teacher addressed me one day by my full name, David LaChapelle, which I thought was strange. I later realized she'd probably done that to tell the girls in the class who I was. I did not even realize it at the time, but my profile and picture were on the Internet because I was registered with a few dating websites. Then, at the end of the course, I had to have a self-addressed envelope so the instructor could mail my final paper to me. That is when the teacher asked if the handwriting on the envelope was my girl-friend's because it was so neat. I told her it was my stepmom's handwriting, and the teacher seemed delighted that I seemed not to have a girlfriend.

Many girls were interested in me at the time, but I was having difficulty responding to people's insights and suggestions. Therefore, while attending the Research Statistics class, I was not myself, and I was going through a transition period. Also, my social skills were poor because I had been isolated for such a long time in Lindsay. This was my first opportunity to interact with others, and it was a scary experience for me.

I thought that my medication impaired my ability to make small talk, so I got it reduced from 6 mg to 4 mg over the summer. I also wanted to reduce my weight. When I moved in with Nancy and Dad, I started putting on weight again. I was on a really strict diet before, but I blame Nancy's good cooking and baking for my weight increase. Nancy would bake scrumptiously delicious pies and cakes. She received such pleasure and enjoyment from feeding you her specialties that it would be a crime to refuse.

It was still summer, and Dad and Nancy went to Edmonton to see my brother, who was transferred from his job in Moncton. I went to the mall to get a haircut, and a new girl cut my hair. I told her that I lived with my parents and that they were in Edmonton for about a week. She invited herself to come over to my place. It was the first time I'd ever met her, and her forwardness threw me off a bit. I ignored what she said and went to the bookstore to buy *Stillness Speaks* by Eckhart Tolle.

The minute I arrived at home, I began reading the book in my bedroom. It did not take long for me to be thrust into the heavenly peace that Eckhart Tolle calls "the Now." I was scared because at that moment I knew there was something more to this life than what I had experienced before. For about eight hours, I lay in my bed with no thoughts, and the eight hours seemed like three minutes. From that moment, I became interested in Eckhart Tolle and his teachings. I looked at life with a different perspective and took that newfound outlook into my second year at Trent.

During the fall term, I took Social Psychology and worked at Home Outfitters and Sears, where I demonstrated the Keurig coffee machine. In Social Psychology, I sat beside a student named Kirsten, who used to sit in front of me in the Research Statistics class. I think Kirsten had a crush on me, but I just wanted to be friends and nothing more. In Social Psychology, we learned things about people and why people do the things they do. The main point I learned was that we all judge others as being better or worse than ourselves. I'd heard of this phenomenon in another book I'd read; it had explained that comparing yourself to others is a sign of poor self-esteem.

The winter term began, and I decided to take two classes: Cognitive Psychology and Personality Theory of Psychology. I learned in Cognitive Psychology that people with Schizophrenia often have poor working memories. Working memory is the memory that sorts through things to pay attention to so that you can put the information into short-term memory or later into long-term memory. I learned in Personality Theory that people with Schizophrenia are often geniuses.

After the winter term ended, I was so lonely. My life had not improved, so I started looking at the employment ads in Toronto because I wanted a life. My dad just laughed at me and told me, "Don't give up with school. Hang in there."

Dad and Nancy realized that I probably needed a change of scenery. They invited my brother and me to join them for three nights in Las Vegas for a vacation. We arrived at the airport at 6:00 a.m. so that we would have ample time to make our morning flight without any hassles.

When I approached US Customs, I became extremely nervous because of my political asylum claim a few years earlier. The customs agent watched me twitch, and sure enough, there I was on his computer. The agent asked, "Have you ever been denied access into the United States?"

I told him, "Yes," and then I added, "I claimed political asylum when I was sick a few years ago."

"Do you have a doctor's note?" he asked.

I told him, "No, I do not have a doctor's note."

We were then escorted to a waiting area to discuss my case. After we waited ten minutes, a customs agent told me, "You have been denied access to the United States."

My father started panicking because our trip was about to be ruined. He asked the customs agent, "Is there anything you can do?"

I kept calm throughout the whole ordeal. Five minutes after the customs agent told me I'd been denied access, a supervisor came out of nowhere and said, "I have good news and bad news."

I said, "OK."

"The good news is you can enter the United States, but the bad news is it will cost you a fee."

I said, "Thank you so much."

And then we were on our way to Vegas.

My brother, flying from Edmonton to Las Vegas, had no clue that we almost did not make it through customs in Toronto.

During my time in Las Vegas, I woke up at 7:00 a.m. and went to bed at 10:00 p.m. One morning around 7:00 a.m., I knocked on my brother's door, and to my surprise he answered the door right away all dressed and ready to go. I thought, *That is unlike my brother to be up so early.*

I asked him, "How come you are up so early?"

He said, "I never went to sleep."

"Wow!" I said.

"I won a $2,500 jackpot, Dave."

I said, "That is great."

"It is not so great because it took me $2,500 to win $2,500."

My brother was a big-time gambler, but I brought only $400 with me.

In Vegas, we saw Carrot Top the comedian and the Cave Man show. We also went to a few shopping malls, where I bought a pair of Tommy Hilfiger jeans, my brother bought some shoes, and my dad bought some sandals. We had a great time.

The last night of our vacation, my brother came to my room all tired around 9:00 p.m.

"Did you win on your Blazing 7's Dollar machine?" I asked.

"I put all my money back in that machine." I'd say he must have deposited about $500 into his machine.

It seemed that he had given up trying to win money, so I said, "Steve, here is $20. Go to your machine, and you will win."

He did not take me up on my offer because he was too tired, so I went to his slot machine, put the $20 into it, and won $200 right away. I then went up to the store and bought some drinks and snacks.

Next, I sat down at a quarter machine for whatever reason. I do not know, but I just had an inclination to sit down at this particular slot machine. I did not want to break into the $200 I had just won, but I did have four $1 bills with me. I thought, *Well, I can afford to part with $4.*

Would you believe that after three or four spins, I won a $600 jackpot? I left Las Vegas a winner and declared on Facebook that I had defeated Sin City.

We returned to Peterborough with a new perspective on life, and we were refreshed. Full of excitement and vigor, I was ready to begin my summer studies at Trent.

I enrolled in Child Development, and Emotion. In Child Development, I learned that when a child always seeks novel things to stimulate him- or herself that is what determines his or her intelligence. When a child grows up, they will seek new challenges and overcome them with ease, because they are used to dealing with problems. In the Emotion class, I learned that we appraise situations twice. During our first appraisal, we judge a situation as being either good or bad, but the second appraisal determines what we do in that particular situation. It was cool to learn about how your emotions operate, and for a while, I was constantly observing my appraisal processes of my emotions. The class made me wonder if a thought precedes an emotion or if an emotion precedes a thought. Also, no matter what mood you are in, if you just smile, you will feel better.

While taking the Emotion course, I became increasingly frustrated by my life circumstances. I was working hard at school, but I had no friends and I was living with my parents. I woke up one morning at 5:00 a.m. and went to sit in the washroom. That is when I felt the heavens opening up and God was lending his ear to me. I felt that God wanted to hear everything I wanted to say, so I made the best of the opportunity. I had never felt more than at that moment that God wanted to listen to what I had to say.

I cried out to God, "What do you expect out of me? I am a human being and I have needs." I added, "Give me a break, and help me out a little." Then I said, "Whatever you are going to do, just move me. I don't care what you do, but make my life different from the way it is now."

The next day, I was sitting in the living room with my dad and Nancy. Dad was complaining to Nancy, "Our house is too small. There is no storage room."

Nancy asked, "Do you want to look at the house that Fran was going to buy?"

That evening, the three of us went to the house that was for sale. It was not far from where we were living. We bought the house on the condition that we sell our house. We moved into the house in July 2009, and I realized that God was truly concerned about my grievances and was listening to me.

I lived in the house on Spillsbury drive for approximately one year. During this time, I was focused on completing my University courses and did not have much else going on in my life. The courses I completed were Human Sexuality, Introduction to Abnormal Psychology, Psychology of Gender, Intimate Relationships, Sleep and Arousal, and Advanced Abnormal Psychology. While I was enrolled in my last two courses, which were Adolescent Development and Family Development, Nancy thought it would be good for me to be living on my own sooner rather than later.

I called Peterborough Housing and told them that I needed to find a place to live. A woman named Tania told me, "Dave, we have affordable apartments for rent. Do you want an application mailed to you?"

I said, "Yes, I would love an application." I was already on the Rent to Geared Income list, but my position at the top of the list expired; three times, I rejected the apartments they offered me because I was satisfied with my living arrangements.

It took a couple of weeks before I was accepted for an apartment in the north end of town. I completed all the paperwork and moved into my new apartment on October 1 2010. It was a shock to have my own apartment after all these years, but I gradually became accustomed to living on my own and greatly enjoyed the benefits of being my own man for a change.

My dad told me I would meet all kinds of people in the building and maybe develop a few friendships. After finishing my fall courses in December 2010, I gradually started developing a social life for myself. I met Mike Waini, a good friend who shares a similar life perspective and enjoys doing the same things. He was a truck driver and was even an ice road truck driver in the Arctic before a doctor told him he could not drive a truck anymore because he had a bad heart.

I hope Mike has many good years ahead of him because he deserves it, just as I deserved to graduate from Trent University in June 2011. At the convocation ceremonies, I had my picture taken with distinguished actor Tom Jackson because he was the chancellor at Trent University.

We are only beginning to uncover the mysteries of Schizophrenia. Who better to do this than individuals with Schizophrenia themselves? The medical community does not completely know what causes Schizophrenia, except that it is a chemical imbalance in the brain. Also, they do not really know how medications work to correct this. I see my illness as something spiritual and a blessing from God to exert his glory, despite its limitations. I have progressed so much from the beginning of my adventure to the present that it is nothing short of a miracle. Even though I received very little treatment from doctors, I did have the support of my family and I took my medication religiously.

I am amazed how one person in your life can change it so dramatically. Angela was such a person for me, as she altered the direction of my life forever. I still do not fully understand what went on between us, but I do know that we were two souls united for a common purpose. That was to free ourselves from our bondage to our egos and the pains and hurts of the past. Angela and I thought that it was others who were the cause of that pain, but we did not realize that the pain was within. Maybe it was caused by some spiritual force or maybe we were just mentally ill? What is mental illness today anyway? Everybody seems crazy, so we are justified in our rightful position in the world. When all is said, I am glad I met Angela, because it was the first time in my life that I had ever met someone who was exactly like me. We were one, and it was beautiful to be together, and wonderful to weave this story together that is now an instrinic part of my life. I hope this story finds a place in your heart as you go about your daily activities and remember that there is more to this illness than meets the eye.

Made in the USA
Charleston, SC
25 July 2012